ANIMAL MINERAL RADICAL

ANIMAL
MINERAL
RADICAL

ESSAYS ON
WILDLIFE,
FAMILY,
AND FOOD

BK LOREN

COUNTERPOINT
BERKELEY

Animal, Mineral, Radical:
Essays on Wildlife, Family, and Food
Copyright © BK Loren 2013

Loren, BK, 1957–
Animal, mineral, radical : essays on wildlife, family, and
food / BK Loren.
p. cm.
ISBN 978-1-61902-073-3 (pbk.)
ISBN 978-1-61902-201-0 (ebook)
1. Contemplation. 2. Nature. 3. Conduct of life. I. Title.
BV5091.C7L668 2013
814'.6—dc23
2012040570

Cover design by Domini Dragoon
Interior design by Tabitha Lahr

COUNTERPOINT
1919 Fifth Street
Berkeley, CA 94710
www.counterpointpress.com

Printed in the United States of America
Distributed by Publishers Group West

10 9 8 7 6 5 4 3 2 1

for Lisa Cech
always has been, always will be

AUTHOR'S NOTE

Most names in these essays have been changed to respect the privacy of the individuals in the stories. Some of the places have been slightly changed if their exact location risks the privacy of the people involved. I strive for complete honesty on the page; however, I have no faith that recollection ever produces an absolute truth. Memory is never perfect, never static, and as far as I can tell, it evolves constantly with age. I'm grateful for that.

CONTENTS

INTRODUCTION

Writing is listening. I have never believed writing has anything to do with having something to say. It always comes to me as listening. It's a little like prayer, I imagine, though I have never leaned toward any religion. But I've been told that, in prayer, there is a moment of asking for something, and then there's a longer period devoted to waiting. That waiting, in and of itself, decreases the desperation and the desire. In it, already, there's a giving up. It throws a person into a state of listening, and—I would guess—the person who asked in the form of prayer begins to see and hear things that make sense in ways that hadn't before asking. In the aftermath, the ragged beauty and reason of everyday life become more lucid. This, to me, is the same process as writing.

If a person comes to writing with "something to say," it risks drowning out this listening and replacing it with verbiage from the ego. I make no claims of lacking ego. But when I write, I pray that ugly beast retreats into its shell and lets something more important emerge.

Each essay in *Animal, Mineral, Radical* grew out of a great deal of silence and listening. At times, this silence-listening was forced on me by a physical illness that wracked my body for over a decade and, on occasion, took away my facility for language altogether. (I talk about this in "Word Hoard," the final essay in this book.) During these years, I was unable to write a word. Then one day, on the almost-other side of the illness, I went for a short run. When I came back from the run I wrote the first three pages of "Trends of Nature." I had never written creative nonfiction before, and I didn't know exactly what the lines I'd written would become—a story? A poem? The form confused me, but I trusted it. I typed one page after the other, and then let the words stand on their own. I didn't worry about form or what I might "do" with the pages. I spent the next few months reading creative nonfiction, studying that form as I had others in the past.

More than ten years after I wrote "Trends of Nature," I've decided to gather a selection of these essays into a book. During this time, the writing world has changed about as much as my body and psyche changed during that long-term illness. When I first started to write again, the Internet was just on the verge of becoming the behemoth it is now. Facebook did not yet exist, CDNow was all the rage, no one had ever twittered a tweet, and a newish company called Amazon had yet to turn a profit. (Though it had been in business since 1994, Amazon's first profit came in 2001.)

But these days the Internet is the center of all media and a focal point of many people's lives. A few mornings ago, I awoke, bypassed the newspaper (as I have done for the past few years), and went straight to my computer for the news.

After I read sections of the *New York Times*, the *Los Angeles Times*, the two local papers, I landed on a smart essay written by the distinguished editors of the literary journal *n+1*. This essay proclaimed that "all contemporary publications tend toward the condition of blogs, and soon, if not yet already, it will seem pretentious, elitist, and old-fashioned to write anything, anywhere, with patience and care."[1]

Though the essay didn't say anything I hadn't read before in some form, its concision and the overall cumulative effect of it and others like it sent me into a week or so of wrestling with what writing means today, what this book can possibly mean to readers. I looked back over the pages, and I remembered what it was like to write again after not being able to write for so long.

During that silent period, what saved me were my daily excursions into nature. I don't mean wilderness. I mean the small patches of nature available to almost everyone, no matter how mannered and procured the land may be. A tree in a planned park is still a tree, and sky will always be sky. Even these small remnants of the wild shifted my consciousness; I slowed down; I breathed differently; I listened, and the process was reminiscent of the days when I was able to write for hours. I felt a palpable connection between the mindfulness required by writing and the mindfulness induced by even the smallest bits of any natural landscape.

About this time I read a book entitled *The Tree*, by John Fowles, first published way back in the predigital age of 1979. It's a heady, tight piece that portrays the writing process as inextricable from the way we view nature. Our collective, cultural attitude toward the natural world, says Fowles, has everything to do with our collective, cultural attitude toward writing and reading. "The danger," says Fowles, "in both art and nature, is that all emphasis is placed on the created, not the creation."[2] We jump to the end product and forget about the lengthy, multidecade process it takes to truly comprehend any art form. In short, he posits the notion that writing—the kind of writing that takes time and patience—is always "in process" and nature is always "in process." Neither is ever finished. The flip side of this reveals that the degree to which we value writing that is *short* on process is on par with the degree to which we devalue the natural world. The "care and patience" that we are willingly forsaking in our approach to language, writing, and reading is directly related to the carelessness and lack of patience we demonstrate collectively—and unconsciously—to the natural world. If we lose "patience and care" in writing and reading, we will lose it in the way we view and interact with nature. Any aesthetic that devalues patience plows the cultural mind-field into fallow ground that begins to tacitly accept the inevitability of oil spills, deforestation, human-induced climate change (global warming), in short, into a consciousness that is linked to, if not synonymous with, the state of mind that allows commerce to take precedence over people and all forms of life.

Collective consciousness matters, and it is not limited to one thing. "It is far less nature itself that is yet in true danger than our attitude to it," said Fowles in 1979.[3] And in the twenty-first century, it is far less literature that is in true danger than our attitude toward it.

I am keenly aware that, as a writer, I am not an anomaly. Most, if not all, working writers take care and patience with their words. But for every careful sentence that a writer labors over into the wee hours of the morning, there is also a professed cultural value for that which is quick, off-the-cuff, and uncrafted. If the editors of *n+1* are right, and "soon, if not yet already, it will seem pretentious, elitist, and old-fashioned to write anything, anywhere, with patience and care," then I hope *Animal, Mineral, Radical* offers a pretentious, elitist veritable fossil of a book.

But, smart and prodigious as their words may be, I think—or maybe, I hope—they'll turn out to be wrong. No doubt we, as a species, have waged (are waging) war on the natural world. For the sake of our survival and that of other living beings, I hope we stop soon. But in the realm of geologic time, the natural world will continue; it will survive, with or without us.

We are currently waging war on language and "literature," a term used fondly in the past and disparagingly these days, implying, as *n+1* says, "elitism." But human trends don't ebb and wane in the same protracted time frame as geology. And I believe in the power of language in the same way I believe in the power of the earth. It will survive. Trite and old-fashioned as it may sound, the human heart will always need words (and work of all kinds) shaped with care and patience, both of which breed compassion. That's what I hope to offer in the pages that follow.

ANIMAL

AS IN WILD, DOMESTIC, ESSENTIAL

TRENDS OF NATURE

A friend of mine says coyotes are passé. He says they've gone the way of the whale. "The whale," he says, "was the first one to make a big splash." He laughs when he says this.

"What was it before whales?" I ask.

"Happy faces. I think it went happy faces, whales, coyotes. But that nature stuff, it's all passé now."

"Oh?"

"Yeah. Now, it's angels."

———————

We were in a desert canyon, and it was the dead of summer, so no one pitched a tent. We, six of us, or so, slept along the banks of a river, most of us lying on top of our sleeping bags. It's one of the simplest, most exhilarating things to do: sleep under the naked sky without a tent, without a sleeping bag, without clothes, if possible. You can feel the stars on your skin. It jump-starts something wild in you, like sticking your finger into a live socket and connecting up with nature. After all, you breathe differently out here. Certain things slow down (your heart rate, the noise in your head), while other things speed up (your awareness, your ability to laugh).

So maybe it was because of how good it feels when there's nothing between you and the sky, but when my eyes peeled open that morning, everything seemed like a hallucination. My friends were sleeping on shore, as they should have been, and the sun was rising, as it does. But there was no separation between earth and sky. What I mean is this: The world felt like an organism, and I was a cell moving through the riparian veins of some single living creature too huge to name. Over there were my friends, buddies on the molecular level, I assumed.

The sky was the color of the inside of a vein: red clouds on the eastern horizon bleeding into white, moving like liquid. The sun pulsed like a huge heart, and everything moved slowly, like lava.

That's when I saw them. In that light, they looked like ghosts. Their legs were longer, skinnier than I'd imagined. The crisp outlines of their scrawny bodies blurred in my sight. There were three of them. Coyotes. Their gait was silent, as if they were not even touching the earth. I might not have believed they existed, except I could see them breathing. I could hear their breath, a certain rhythm almost like panting, but less desperate, more quiet.

It takes a while for the brain to file information straight from nature. You don't expect it. No matter how many times you go out into the woods, you don't expect to see wild animals this close to you. At first, they loped. Then they crouched and lowered their heads, sniffing toward my sleeping friends. *I should warn everyone*, I thought. One coyote wouldn't have posed too much of a threat, but three might have come up with a way to slow human population growth in their canyon. But I was not recognizing this sight as "reality." I felt as if my dreams had seeped out of my brain and their images were pouring into my waking life: *This* was an illusion.

I remained motionless. And the light of the morning changed from soft reds to a brilliant dome of blue burned through by a hot dime of white sun.

The coyotes vanished as the day began. It was as if they knew I was on the verge of believing they were real, so they teased my tenuous grasp of reality and disappeared. Suddenly, one coyote stopped and looked up. They all stood at attention for a second, then ran. The way they ran made me certain I'd been hallucinating because I couldn't track them. There was nothing tricky about it. They didn't take some wild and hidden path. They just vanished. I can't tell you where they went. If they had gone up the sides of the canyon, as I thought, why wasn't I able to see them as they loped away? It was as if they entered the walls of the canyon, the way the dead baseball players in *Field of Dreams* entered the cornfields—except, better. A lot better.

Eventually, my friends woke up, and while it was great to be outdoors, there was nothing dreamlike about the day. We ate breakfast the way river runners eat breakfast: eggs, milk, coffee, hash browns, pancakes, French toast, syrup, orange juice, tortilla chips, salsa, beans, et cetera. We didn't scrimp. We celebrated and indulged. After all, this was nature. This was home. It would be weeks before we saw the inside of an office building or a shopping mall.

Everyone is allowed to be in any mood they want in a place like this, and I was quiet that morning. I couldn't shake the image of the coyotes, but for some reason, I didn't want to tell my friends about them. I still felt like some particulate matter floating inside a monstrous creature. I don't know why the coyotes affected me this way; they just did. I kept repeating the word *lope* to myself. My tongue leaned from the *l* into the *oohh* then fell softly onto the *pah* of the *p*. *Lope*. It sounded like coyotes to me, the way their thin legs moved, the way their paws stopped with a *pah* on the soft earth. *Lope*. *Lope*.

That's how I paddled my kayak that morning. My shoulder was loose and relaxed. My paddle tilled the water softly. The river was calm, class 2 all day. And I was a coyote. Or, more accurately, I was a human with the arrogance to believe that for a few hours before noon on that day, I moved with some sort of animal grace. Truth was, I couldn't get their beauty out of my mind. They moved like every perfection I'd ever strived to attain. Yet they were anything but perfect. They just were.

Like anything wild.

After the river trip ended and I returned home to Taos, a pack of coyotes began trotting by my home at twilight. My windowsill was level with the ground, no screen attached, so the coyotes would stick their heads inside, sniff curiously, then continue into the night. My roommate would squirt them with water to scare them away, but I enjoyed their visits. When I was alone in the house, I just greeted them and wished them a prosperous hunt.

When I landed a job in Northern California, I bid the pack and their new spring pups farewell and moved on.

I entered another time zone upon my arrival on the West Coast. I'd picked Santa Cruz because I'd heard it was a "laid-back town." When I lived Taos, businesses, even banks, closed on whim. If you wanted the day off, you didn't call in sick; you called up your fellow employees, and you all took a few days off. Customers would return another day. The weather, an ephemeral thing, was beautiful. That took precedence.

This wasn't the way in California. It turns out, *laid-back* referred to a style of dress, not a way of life. Coffee was essential to survival. Putting in fifty hours a week, I was a slacker.

Add this to the commute. I couldn't afford a place "close in," so I drove forty miles to work each morning, along with thousands of other ants. The colony gathered just after dawn, and by seven, we were head-to-butt in line, gassing our cars and SUVs into the Silicon Valley, where we'd spend the day in smaller colonies working fast and hard, talking faster and harder, before returning home via the same frantic route to enjoy whatever thin slice of evening remained.

A month of this, and I was spent. I decided to start my commute before dawn to avoid traffic. I didn't drive fast. I sauntered. I pondered the redwoods ensconced in ocean mist making the forest look two-dimensional—black-and-white, shadowed. When the sun poured over the hills and the fog lifted, the whole place turned to a labyrinth of red spires draped with green.

But at least once a week I overslept, skipped breakfast, slammed down coffee, jockeyed my way over the hill, and sprinted to my eight o'clock class, tests and essays flying from my briefcase and my students already in their seats awaiting my presence. My wimpish ability to adopt a California pace set my circadian rhythms to twitching like chiggers beneath my skin. I was living in a blur of a world that passed by so fast I couldn't wrap my fingers around anything certain, and I'd grown addicted to the adrenaline rush that accompanied this pace. My car was an extension of myself, and I never thought twice about it until my car and I, speeding over Highway 17, killed a coyote.

She was the first coyote I'd seen in California. And in the split second when I first saw her, I remembered the ghostlike grace of the pack I'd seen by the river. Though I'd seen scores of other animals in the wild, coyotes always seemed to me as if they'd risen straight out of the earth, like phantoms. But this one was not an apparition, not a hallucination. My eyes connected with hers, and there was no time to move my foot from gas pedal to brake. She emerged from behind the concrete highway divider, looked through my windshield, lost, sniffing toward me, and my car barreled into her.

Still alive, she tumbled over the hood and into the steady stream of traffic behind me. Several other cars struck her before she landed on the shoulder of the highway. I watched this through my rearview mirror as I tried to change lanes and cut my way to the side of the road. Traffic never slowed.

Sometimes when I tell this story, I talk about how I immediately parked my car and walked to the coyote's side. I explain the fear I felt as I approached a wounded animal, something I'd been told was dangerous. I tell the story of how her eyes turned toward me, how I could hear her breath, fast and shallow, like small wings.

I say, "I wondered if she was smelling me the way animals smell, the way they take in information through air, if she could smell her own death on me as I stood there, watching her die."

But the gap between the story I tell and what actually happened is equal to the gap between who I wanted to be and who I'd become.

I did stop. The next morning.

Night haunted me. All the possibilities of what I would have seen and felt if I'd watched her die and known I had killed her played like a film in my head. But the thing that got to me most was that the reason I was feeling anything at all was pure ego. This was the coyote *I* killed. *I* was on my way to work. *I* didn't stop. *I* could have stopped. I made myself sick.

What about the scores of coyotes—and other animals—I'd seen strewn along roadsides before? Why did it take my direct participation in a death to push me to the point of change? Why, in that moment, did I decide to move closer to my work and start riding a bicycle everywhere? Why didn't the years of carnage I'd seen have any real effect on me?

For weeks afterward, I felt caught. Not caught doing something wrong, but caught doing something I had not chosen to do. Peer pressure: simple as that. When I saw the spark of brown eyes framed by clumps of blondish-gray fur, the ears cocked like a quizzical pup's, the graceful stride, the familiar lope, it was like retrieving a huge part of myself. For a split second, I remembered who I was. And then I saw myself driving fast, cutting people off, flipping that middle finger proudly, as if the marks of good character were summed up in a fast car, quick driving reflexes, and making a forty-minute drive in under thirty. So when the coyote emerged, I couldn't stop. I killed her.

<hr />

The next morning I left before dawn. I drove slowly. When I reached the coyote's body, I stopped. I wish I could say I was overcome with guilt, or anger, or fear. Any emotion would have been good. But I wasn't overcome with anything. For the first time in my life I felt what it meant to be numb. It began in the marrow of my bones and radiated outward. It wasn't that I felt nothing. I felt everything at once and everything became a wall of emptiness that separated me from who I'd planned to be.

—•◦•—

It took a while to find a place to live closer to work. Until then, I watched the coyote's body decompose as I drove over the hill every morning. First it stiffened, then bloated. Then parasites and scavengers devoured her muscles, and her blond-gray fur was blown away by wind.

—•◦•—

When I run along the paved trails carved through City Open Space, I think of the Nacirema, a "North American group living in the territory between Canadian Cree, the Yaqui and Tarahumare of Mexico, and the Carib and Arawak of the Antilles." They were a "culture characterized by a highly developed market economy which evolved in a rich natural habitat,"[1] and "the Nacirema considered it of primary importance to completely remake the environment of the lands they occupied."[2] No natural place was sacred until it was transformed. Trees were okay, as long as they didn't grow in their native settings. Where there was desert, the Nacirema brought in water and created lakes and models of oceans. In time, they say, the Nacirema might have sought to alter the stars and sun. They worshipped unnatural light.

So I figure the Nacirema must have paved these Open Space trails, and I'm grateful for the little bit of nature they allow in my city. They're wonderful for a quick jog. Mornings, I sprint past the tennis courts, picnic tables, and barbecues, then I turn eastward and travel alongside a water canal that I pretend is a natural river. Here, I've seen cormorants, kestrels, a variety of hawks and chickadees. The place brims with life.

Recently, however, the houses along this stretch have begun breeding at an unreasonable rate. The oversized embryos develop each time I see them. First, there are the pine poles flagged with red surveyor's tape, a housing developer's announcement of estrus. Once these are up, you know the land will be fucked. Next, the wooden skeletons form, followed by the foil-covered, fatty layer of insulation. Then the hammers begin palpitating, echoing an off-beat rhythm through the empty air.

Sometimes, to avoid watching this unrestrained propagation, I look only at my feet as I run. I concentrate on my breathing. I put on blinders.

That's how I was running that afternoon. There was no reason to look up. But for some reason, I did. I looked up in that way you do when you know you're about to run into something—a pole, another person, a wild animal.

I gasped, and that banal utterance "Oh my god" slipped through my lips. By now, I was familiar with every curve and outline of a coyote. But I didn't expect to find one here, and I don't think he expected to find himself here, either. It was a young male. He stood about five feet in front of me, right in the middle of the path. I didn't know what to do. I just stared. The coyote just stared. Then he shifted his gaze from one side to the other.

My eyes followed his. To the north, those houses were breeding like humans. To the south, the city was installing a golf course.

I know a wild animal is wild and anything suggesting otherwise is a fairy tale. When the gates of Eden finally swung open, the animals made a firm decision. They fled, never again to befriend the creature responsible for destroying paradise. But what I saw in that animal's eyes was not wildness, or at least, not as we've come to know it. I took a step toward the coyote. He didn't move, but shifted his eyes again. Then he looked back at me and tilted his head. One of us had to move, and I think he wanted it to be him. But he didn't know where to go.

I'm reading all of this into the languageless space between the coyote and me, of course. But what else can explain that he compromised with me? As I passed, he sidestepped just enough to let me by. He never snarled, or even lowered his head. My heart pounded—with exhilaration? Fear? I don't know.

I ran backwards for a while so I could watch what he would do next. He stayed in that spot for as long as I watched. Then my path rounded a bend.

When I returned a few minutes later, he was gone. Crusty snow blanketed a nearby ravine, and I saw his tracks, but not where they led. I didn't want to see where they led. I wanted him to live out his life there. I hoped no one would ever find him. I hoped his small space would remain wild.

Recently the "proliferation" of coyotes in our area has made headlines. Coyotes have been sighted on bicycle trails and walking paths. According to news sources, they've become a problem.

Yesterday morning from my kitchen window I watched a pack return from their hunt. They ran across the field in a cloud of dust, then dropped behind the berm near the horse stables. The horses raised their heads and scattered for a moment, the contrails of their breath rising in the morning air. Then they went back to grazing.

When I first moved to this neighborhood, I spoke to a woman who said she was feeding coyotes in her backyard. I suggested this might not be a good idea.

"But they have puppies," she said. Her husband was the man who told me coyotes are "passé."

"We see coyotes so often now, they're really overexposed," he said. "The hot trend today is angels."

I took his statement to mean that the popular trend of nature as commodity has descended; the thing today is angels—beautiful, ethereal beings who grant quick miracles. They hover above the earth, are not born of soil, and come from a place more "heavenly" than ours.

I try to conjure the image of an angel and a place more beautiful than earth. But I see them again, the ghostlike outlines of those graceful coyotes loping by the river where I lay perfectly naked beneath the round sky before dawn.

THE SHIFTING LIGHT
OF SHADOWS

'd seen ghosts of them now and then: the recently cleaned spine of a deer lying on a mountainside, bloodied ribs reaching up from the ground like fingers trying to hold on to empty air; on another day, a carcass so fresh I thought it was an injured deer lying with its head on a rock. I began walking toward it but stopped when I saw the shiny dark flask of the stomach removed and placed prominently on a nearby rock, ravens beginning to gather above it. I thought better of my approach then.

I spent one winter tracking them as part of my job at Eldorado Canyon State Park. That's when I learned that mountain lions crave fresh meat so much, they will not eat the predigested stench wrapped in the stomach of their kill. Cats are finicky eaters. They carry the stomach away, like an offering to the needier scavengers. I also learned to walk very upright as I tracked. I knew that bending down to, say, pick up a rock because I thought I heard a lion nearby was not a good idea. It would have turned my two legs into four, giving any nearby lion a familiar line of sight up my spine to my neck. A lion is generally stymied by the teetering, Humpty-headed stature of two-leggeds—perhaps one reason why attacks on humans are so rare.

I always presumed I was in the presence of a lion when tracking. There are just too many cats in the foothills of Boulder, and too many signs to believe anyone ever walks alone here. Still, during those six months of steadily following cougars, I never saw even the tail of a cat as it ran away, never saw a distant lion pacing on a far-off cliff or heard one caterwauling under the shivering Colorado stars, though nearby residents said they heard lions almost every night. No doubt, lions were watching me as I searched for them with my comparatively feeble eyes. I probably looked right at a cat. But I never saw one.

I never thought a tennis court would be the place. Imagine the "What to Do If You Encounter a Mountain Lion Here" instructions. *Make yourself look big. Face the lion, and don't turn your back. Never serve, but always volley if served to. Avoid running for the ball; this could spur the lion's chasing instinct. Keep your eye on the ball. A lion could take direct eye contact as a full-court challenge.*

It would be pretty unlikely to see a wild cat striding across that smooth green surface where, earlier in the day, Edgar and George, vacationing from Texas, donned white shorts and Ts and ran with their creaky, sixty-year-old knees, on their spindly hairless legs, chasing bright yellow balls and calling, "Good shot, cowboy."

But predictability is not any big cat's strong suit. My first sighting of the lions native to my Colorado home was on a tennis court in the Boulder foothills. I was staying in what I have come to call "my office"—a cabin I use in Chautauqua Park when I need a little extra solitude for writing. After work that night, I'd walked into town with my partner for dessert, and on the way back we were feeling good. We'd had some kind of gooey chocolate caramel ice cream thing and a split of champagne, and we were, maybe, a little bit buzzed. We were certainly oblivious, but no less so than the average person coming home, unlocking the door, and entering the house. It's just one of those annoying human tendencies—to ignore where we are most of the time. As we rounded the corner to the cabin, though, that common obliviousness vanished. Lisa stopped talking midword and tugged my sleeve. "Look," she said. I thought she was pointing to the silhouettes of two great horned owls sitting in the ponderosa pine. I looked up, but she tugged again, harder this time, and I looked down— and I saw it in the spotlight of the green tennis court: a mountain lion.

I've seen bears in the wild before and have often mistaken them for something else on first glance. My mind, an unfortunate stranger to wild animals, clicks in and says, "Hey, that's one huge dog, one strange-looking deer, a very fat black house cat" (the cubs).

It was not this way with the mountain lion. It was unequivocally, distinctly, and immediately *a lion*.

Even though that recognition struck me with certainty, it was hard to discern the figure of the cat. I'd spent six months looking for this creature. I had begun to believe in mountain

lions the way some people believe in God. I knew they existed, but I'd given up finding anything other than circum-
stantial evidence. I never imagined meeting one in the flesh.
Stunned, I watched the cougar cross the court, crouched,
shoulder blades jutting from its back like the jagged slabs of
rock it had emerged from. I guessed it was a male, weighing
in at about 150 pounds of pure muscle. Even carrying all that
bulk and power, it looked afraid. It looked as if it knew it was
in unfriendly territory. It prowled along a decidedly precise
path, as if it had a specific place to go and it regretted having to cross the tennis court to get there. It turned its head
slightly from side to side as it slunk across the concrete, then
leapt—all 150 pounds of it—soundlessly up onto the specta-
tor's ledge. It passed between two houses and emerged onto
the street, caught between the headlights of a car and a group
of teenagers.

It was anything but aggressive. It hunched down and away
from the headlights, like a house cat confronted with a mighty
vacuum cleaner. With the car clearly in its line of travel, it had
nowhere to go, so it turned and followed the teens, walked
within ten or fifteen yards of them, and the second it saw an
escape route, it vanished. I didn't *see* its escape route. Simply,
the cat was there, and then it wasn't. My eyes couldn't follow
it. No sign of it remained in its wake.

I wish I could say I walked quietly back to my cabin, let
the whole event sink in as I sat by the fire, contemplating the
animal's beauty. I didn't do anything as cool and enlightened

as that. Instead, I celebrated like a fool. I had finally caught sight of something I'd been looking for for years, something sublime. I was exuberant. I called out to the kids, "Hey, did you know there was a mountain lion right behind you a second ago?"

A boy looked over his shoulder. "What?"

"A mountain lion!"

The whole gang glanced back at me nonchalantly. Then they burst out laughing. "Right," one of them said. One of them started imitating a mountain lion; then he stood up and they all laughed and went on about their nighttime carousing. It was as if they couldn't fathom that something wild had been that close to them.

I couldn't sleep that night. I woke every hour or so, looked out to the tennis court. When I did sleep, I dreamed of the lion over and over. In my dreams, it was less shadowy, more familiar. It seemed at home there, in my sleeping brain, where all sorts of impossibilities become real, even though the reality of them vanishes in the light of day.

———

I spent a few years studying at the C. G. Jung Institute of Colorado in Denver. In Jung's theory of dreams, the deeper, most complex layer of consciousness is the collective unconscious. The images it holds (archetypes) are, theoretically, common to us all. According to Jung, a particularly powerful dream probably has roots in the collective unconscious. In its logical extreme, the collective unconscious is not bound by time nor limited to humans. It suggests that we are all one—a notion that in Jung's day had not been diluted by pop culture and New Age thought as it is today. It changed the course of psychological inquiry. Dreams, Jung said, are the doorway to the personal and the collective unconscious, and the degree to which we achieve individuation (which is not as much about becoming an "individual" as it is about becoming whole) is equal to the degree to which we integrate the unconscious.

The cat came to me like a dream, like a door to another world, a world so foreign and distant that I stumbled over the threshold of it; a world so familiar and integral to who I am, maybe to who we all are, that I longed for it. It was not a sentimental longing. It felt like the recognition of something necessary, not of a romantic accouterment.

One of the most well-known of Jung's archetypes is the Shadow. It is often misinterpreted as solely the negative side of the Self: the *potential* for each and every one of us to be everything that we fear in others, from self-absorbed and snotty, to liars and thieves, even murderers. And while all that unsavory stuff *is* true about the Shadow, the Shadow also holds within it all our internal repressed fears that are *positive*: the part of us that may be afraid of success, or of being loved, or of losing our temper. Or of the very daunting possibility of becoming whole.

It seems more than coincidental that the mountain lion is often called the Shadow Cat. It is nocturnal. It shows itself when most of the people in the houses near its territory are dreaming. To ranchers and owners of livestock, it is sometimes viewed as a thief. Cats are often portrayed as mysterious, not to be trusted. Even more often, they are seen as killers, and it is becoming more and more likely that because of this, they will be killed (and we, the killers).

It's the most natural response one has when confronted with the archetype of the Shadow. Mountain lions embody what we fear and despise about ourselves, and we seek to eradicate it. We view it as *other*—unwanted and unnecessary.

But eradicating the Shadow, rather than integrating it, would mean a breakdown of the personality. And eradicating the mountain lion from the wilderness would cause a breakdown of what remains of that wilderness, to say nothing of the effects it would have, consciously or unconsciously, on the human psyche. (*Psyche*, in Greek, means soul.) Annihilate all that you hate and fear, and it takes with it all that you love and desire.

It's not any more "New Agey" to say that cats are symbolic to Americans than it is to say the eagle is symbolic. If the eagle has come to symbolize some collective sense of "freedom," the cat has come to symbolize solitary strength, self-awareness (awareness even in darkness), keeping to one's boundaries (the way a female lion defends her territory); it symbolizes the heart of the wilderness we all need and desire—the wilderness that is shrinking beneath us, unconsciously, like a dream forgotten upon waking.

———•◦◆◦•———

The next morning when I went to the lodging office to check out of my cabin, I mentioned to Kathleen, the concierge, that I'd seen a mountain lion on the tennis court. Kathleen and I had become friendly since I began staying in the Chautauqua cabins; but as soon as the words left my lips, I wished I'd kept them to myself. I'm not a religious person. But I'd witnessed, the night before, a messenger from a place I hold to be divine: the wilderness. True wilderness is pretty much gone now, but a remnant of it remains in something as wild as a mountain lion.

After I spoke to Kathleen, I walked downtown, and I knew that my world had somehow been shifted in the same subtle but certain way it shifts in the aftermath of a powerful dream. Likewise, to describe that shift would be as impossible as explaining the impact of a dream.

I can only describe it like this: I walked into my favorite coffee shop–bookstore and took a seat at a table where someone had left a stack of books. On top was a slender volume entitled *Caught in Fading Light*, and it had on its cover the dusky outline of a cougar. It told the story of the author, Gary Thorp, tracking one specific mountain lion daily for over a year and never seeing it.

Jung would call the appearance of that book on the table where I sat after seeing a cougar *synchronicity*, two events connected by something stronger than chance. I didn't call it anything. If I'd been in another state of mind, it might have impressed me. That day, it just made sense. Just as it made sense that the next book in the stack was by Rainer Maria Rilke, and when I turned to the first page my eyes fell on a poem called "Archaic Statue of Apollo." In this poem, Rilke is struck silent by a sight so beautiful and unfathomable that it shifts his world. To him, it was a statue of an ancient god, an archetype. In the presence of the piece of art, Rilke sees everything that is possible in him, but that he has not yet become. The last few lines of the poem are

> *Otherwise the shoulders*
> *would not glisten like the fur of a wild animal:*
> *would not, from all the borders of itself,*
> *burst like pure light: for here there is no place*
> *that does not see you. You must change your life.*

———

Rilke, nearly a full century ago, called upon the image of a wild animal to illustrate the peaceful yet powerful strength that comes to us rarely and shifts our world. The possibility of it exists in all of us. It is the dream of a common language that harks back through history and provides a connection between us all. Here, there is no place that does not *see* you.

I finished my drink, bought both books, and, well, as soon as I left the place the mundane world wiggled its way back into my life. My cell phone rang. On the end of the line was a park ranger. "We have a report of a lion sighting in Chautauqua," the ranger said.

"Yes, I saw a lion."

"It stalked some teenagers?"

"It didn't stalk them," I said. "It walked behind them, looking for a place to go. It acted just like a lion should act. It was a good lion, a *good* lion." I knew that any behavior illustrating this cat had grown too used to humans could label it a "bad cat" and put the animal at risk.

Though I knew that Kathleen had done the right thing by reporting my sighting (the cougar was on the tennis court, after all), it also felt somehow wrong to me. Maybe my personal unconscious understood the need for monitoring a large predator's behavior, especially when people had chosen to live smack-dab in the middle of the predator's habitat. But at the same time, something in me, maybe my collective unconscious, wanted that cat to remain untouched by human eyes, uncontrolled by rangers, and completely wild.

The conversation I had with the ranger edged too close to an absurd moment I'd experienced in my little suburban home. I was out one morning at dawn, working in the garden, when a red fox emerged from the blond, dried grasses in the open field behind my house. I stopped, leaned on my shovel, and fell momentarily in love with that fox. With its long, lean body, its bushy coat, the red that deepens to black on the tip of the tail—oh, yes, it really was love. Just then, an SUV pulled up to the stop sign on my corner. The driver caught sight of the fox, too, and her jaw dropped. Her window was down, so I waved and called out to her, "Gorgeous, huh?" She picked up her cell phone and put it to her ear. I thought, *What an unfortunate time to receive a phone call, right when she could be taking in the sight of this magnificent fox running across the field at dawn.*

She looked frantic, though. I figured she'd received up-setting news on the phone, something that sent her into a near panic. So I picked up my shovel and walked closer to see if I could help. She rolled down the window and almost screeched at me. "Did you see that *animal?*" she said.

"Yes." I kept up my bright smile.

"Good, good. I'm calling animal control right now. They'll take care of it," she said.

I wondered at the fear bubbling up so readily inside her, and at her trust in something—a phone call—that could so easily put that fear in check.

Luckily, my conversation with the ranger turned out to be nothing like my conversation with my neighbor. I had feared it might, until I realized, in true "Shadow form," that this ranger was doing exactly what I had done when I worked for Eldorado Canyon State Park. At the end of the conversation, she said, "Yeah, we know that lion, or at least we know *of* it.

It has a kill over on the north side of the mountain. It was no doubt just heading out for its dinner."

Jung once said, "One does not become enlightened by imagining figures of light, but by making the darkness conscious."[1]

If the lion, in all its dark, nocturnal otherness, in all its light, internal sameness, does not exist for future generations, if we destroy its habitat, or call open season on it, what could we possibly find to replace it? It is precisely *because* we fear large predators that we need them. They hold within them so many things we have lost, or are on the verge of losing, personally and collectively, permanently and forever. If we sacrifice the fear, we also sacrifice the strength, the wildness, the beauty, the awe.

In those few seconds when I was in the presence of the lion, I did not say to myself, "You must change your life." I knew, right then and there, that my life had been changed. A piece of something necessary had clicked into place inside me. I had become more aware, more intimate with my own fear and my own possibilities. I remembered what it was like to be humbled by awe. I became more compassionate. I became a better person.

OF STRAW DOGS AND CANINES:
A MEDITATION ON PLACE

Coyotes are consummate illusionists. Take a western land-scape, a few piñon pines gnarled like arthritic knuckles, chamisa blooming like handfuls of sunlight, mesas mirages in the distance, and there, on that wide horizon, they will materialize. Where there was nothing now there is something, long-legged, loping. They give you their tough-guy glance, and panting, they move on. You barely believe you've seen them before they sink back into the earth. You think of the word *vanish* and understand the sound of it now: the hard *V* at the beginning, the hush by the time it ends, how quickly something comes to nothing.

The Hubble Telescope pointed its powerful lens at a bigger expanse of nothingness than any poet's wasteland could ever define, and more than ten thousand galaxies appeared, seventy-eight billion light years away, the distant past of them emerging before our eyes in a place that was once empty.

Place is never empty.

When I was a kid, my brother told me the Rocky Mountains surrounding our home were wolves, their jagged shoulder blades hunched up, heads lowered. Their coats changed with the seasons: snow white in winter, granite gray in summer. But to me the mountains looked like a sleeping dragon. The crags to the north: the spiny tail. The lumpy hogbacks to the south: the dragon's snout. I have always needed stories. Mountains were my first stories. They've been telling my life over and over ever since.

Now I am a writer, and I understand characters as bodies of land; they rise up from place like coyotes, like mountains, like me. I see the red dirt of Colorado, and it looks like the marrow of my bones: gritty, rust-colored mud.

Without place, all stories become weightless, their characters dangling from dog-eared pages, hoping for a word to give them marrow, bone, body. Even the way we speak is formed by wind whistling across certain landscapes, the words of New Yorkers streetwise enough to turn corners too early, dropping *rs* as they run to grab a cab; and the voice of a rural girl saying *haa-ay*, making it two syllables, as if she had all the time in the world.

Without place, every sentence is from nowhere.

For years after I'd grown, after my parents died, I lived in my childhood home. Over my lifetime, the small field behind the house had become a Hubble galaxy. On first glance: some land. Years later: the migrations of birds I knew better than any calendar could predict, down to the day—Swainson's hawks in mid-March, barn swallows in May. The turn of the day ticked in my ears like the rhythms of wings flying home.

Night saturated me: howls of coyotes in the field, wind skittering across the pond, predawn meadowlarks singing. The sound of the nearby train rumbled through my sleep, a comfort, not an intrusion.

When I am embraced in place, I don't need to buy anything to organize my life. Each step appears in the sway of the day. I don't need anything to fill me. I sense what is possible, my day brimming with discovery where there was once familiarity, the land a palimpsest that layers with time.

The pretense that place does not matter turns us all into straw dogs subjected to the whims of marketing. If we are unattached, we need. We need so many things to ground us. If we point the lens into the core of us and no galaxy appears, then what? We dangle, storyless, bland words rolling across the windy landscapes of our tongues. We stay awake all hours of the night, peering out windows until, at last, we let go of longing and accept the constellations that connect us all. We rest our eyes on a horizon that tells a story from the bones out, embraces us from the skin in, lets us rise from the dust of where we've been and where we are, like coyotes, hunting, hungry, finally knowing exactly what it is that feeds us.

MINERAL

AS IN SOLID, CRYSTALLINE,
INTERLOCKED, CREATING A
SOMETIMES JAGGED BOND

MARGIE'S DISCOUNT

My mother loves a good bargain. We're in the designer section of the department store where she worked for two decades. She says, "Don't you like this one better?" She holds up a blouse.

I counter with another blouse. "This one's the same, but it's ten dollars cheaper."

She tucks her own find under her arm and approaches me. She looks at the label, then the price tag. She holds high the blouse she picked out. "This is a *Liz*," she says in the same way I might say, "This is by *Faulkner*." My mother points to the seams, explaining the underground world of designer clothes to me. "Liz clothes last forever. And look, this used to be fifty-six dollars and it's marked down to twenty-five, plus my discount."

"Do you get a discount here?" I say, teasing her because "Plus my discount" has been her mantra for the past two hours of shopping, as it is her mantra whenever we shop at Joslin's, where she worked for years.

"Yes, I get a discount," she says, in the same way I might say, "Officer, I did not run that red light," with indignity and a hint of doubt, even though I really did not run the light. She adds, in a whisper, "And I get an extra 15 percent on my VIP card."

My mother wears hats, has a virtual stockroom of shoes (bought on sale), and lives in a mobile home. She's built a little like a tree if the tree could be a redwood and a willow simultaneously, with a strength and rootedness accumulated over time, with a pliability and grace that bend with care for those around her.

Although I can't put a finger on what it is, there's a quality to the expression on her face that pinches my emotions. It's an expression that remains even when she's relaxed. One eyebrow is higher than the other, sharply arched; the other brow curves softly, the eye underneath it more open, more innocent. This asymmetry gives her the constant look of confusion. Not the confusion of one who does not understand the world, but rather, of one who understands, but perceives something is wrong. The expression has been there since she was a child. I've seen it in old photos: Margie and her brother, Bill, standing by the dairy cart; Margie and Bill proudly holding a stick with two or three trout dangling from it; Margie holding her handmade rag doll; and later, Margie holding her first child, her second, her third, her fourth. She is my mother, the woman with the eyebrows unevenly arched, the eyes that suspect everything and are simultaneously innocent in every moment.

This month is my birthday. Though I am in my forties now, my mother will shower me with gifts, and as I unwrap them, she will say, "Guess how much I paid for that?" I will not need to guess high in order to satiate her appetite for bargains. She will have given me the best of the best for the least of the least. She will look at me with the eyes that tell two stories. She will say, "Open this one next."

⁂

I don't remember when the love of a good bargain overtook my mother's life. She was free of the condition when I was a kid. My earliest memories are of her rising in total darkness, putting on tights and a T-shirt, and exercising. I sat on the sofa with my legs curled into my chest and watched as she raised her arms to the ceiling and touched her toes, once, then again. She did backbends and knee bends. She sat on the floor, stretched her legs into a *V*, and held out her hands.

"Row with me," she'd say. And I'd lower myself from the too-big sofa, sit on the floor, stretch my legs out, place my feet on the inside of her knees. She'd grasp my hands, and we'd row back and forth, then bend at the waist and circle to the side, back, and forward again, around and around. With her legs in almost-Russian splits, my mother could touch her chest to the floor. She didn't do push-ups on her knees. She ran three miles a day before Nike told her she needed a special shoe to do so. She did all this in the silence before dawn. By eight in the morning, she looked like anybody else's mother, smearing peanut butter on two pieces of Wonder Bread, licking grape jelly from her thumb, patting meat and bread crumbs into a loaf for dinner, wearing an apron, opening the

screen door halfway to check on me or to wave hello to another kid's mom.

I'm sharing her ritual with her these day, not the shopping,
but the workouts. I get up at five, put on my sweats, and lug
my gym bag to the car. When I arrive at my mom's place, she's
sitting on the porch, the half light of dawn shadowing her,
making her look even smaller than her five-foot-three frame.
She waves from beneath the eaves and comes out wearing a
red tam cocked to one side of her head.

"You don't have to wait outside for me, Mom," I say. "It's
dark."

She says, "I wasn't waiting long. I heard your car."

As she slides into the car seat, I think of the avocets. I've
been riding my bike to a marshy pond where they stand in
the bent morning sun, their long, amber necks sometimes
shadowed, sometimes gilded in the light, their black wings
like precise pencil etchings on their white shoulders. I think
of them not because my mother resembles them in any real
way, but because she is graceful and quiet beneath her body
that appears to some to be growing awkward with age, her
mind that will not still from worry.

She says, "I know what you're thinking. You're thinking I'm
deaf in one ear, so I couldn't have heard your car. But I did. You
always drive in on my good side." She points to her hearing ear.

"Are you riding the bike today?" I ask.

"Yes. I went 10.8 miles last time. I'll go 11 today."

In the gym, I take my place on a treadmill behind my mom's stationary bicycle. I watch as her feet pedal in circles, and as I run, I can feel the rain that fell on us the day we rode mountain bikes in Crested Butte when she was sixty. My memory keeps clicking backward, her odometer, forward. I close my eyes, let my memory go. But shortly, my mother pokes me. "I did it," she says. She's standing beside me, pointing to the bike odometer. "Eleven miles."

"Good job, Mom." I stop the treadmill and follow her to the weights. We look like retired boxers, our sweaty towels hanging around our necks. She places the pin under the sixty-five-pound plate. I spot her. I watch her left arm tremble, her right arm remain steady as she lifts.

"That's the same weight I lift, Mom."

"You better work harder then." She laughs and spots me as I lift.

———◦•✦•◦———

Though my mother is strong, there are two challenges that inevitably defeat her: She cannot allow herself to sleep more than five hours a night, and she cannot remain quiet when she's feeling an emotion. This is not to say she speaks about the emotion. Rather, it goes like this: After we work out, it is tradition to have tea and toast at my house. As we enter, my mother sees a photo of my grandmother, her mother, on my coffee table. "Is that a picture of Mom?" she says.

"Yes. I was going through old photo albums."

My mother pauses for some time, both physically and verbally, then, referring to her mother's premature death, she says, "I never got a chance to thank her." She stands motionless.

"She knew," I say. "Like you know how grateful I am to you."

Her eyes well up, then zero in on the living room carpet. "Is that spot from one of the dogs?" she says. She walks quickly into the kitchen, returns with a wet rag, kneels down, and starts scrubbing. It takes me five minutes to convince her to join me in the kitchen. "I'll be in in just a minute," she says, her voice cracking. After tea is served and the toast is hot and buttered, her bent body rounds the corner. She's fighting the emotion still; I can tell by the way she focuses on the rag and talks incessantly. "I think I got most of it. You might check it later. When things are wet you can't tell for sure if they're stains or . . ." She takes a seat by the window, her audible stream of consciousness like a river during spring runoff.

"I got a positive response from the agent I told you about," I say.

"The one in New York?" she says.

"Yes. I'm going there Friday to meet her."

"Going where?"

"New York."

She stares out the window. She looks hard at the horses in the field behind my home that used to be her home. She looks as if she is trying to remember something. She fails.

"Why are you going to New York?" she asks.

I reiterate. She remains quiet and places her right hand on her left to still the tremble.

———————

The doctors tell my mother she has the heart of a child, 60 strong beats a minute at rest, 130 on the cardio machines and she's not even maxed. She was eating sprouts and yogurt when the rest of America was drowning in mayo and iceberg lettuce. The doctors tell my mother, "You're in great shape." She comes home and says, "I don't have Parkinson's. The doctors say I'm in great shape."

"You can be in great shape and have Parkinson's." I bark this sentence at her like a Doberman, then I hate myself for being the one who must remind her of her disease. Occasionally, I hate her for having it, then I hate myself more, and it goes on like this until I accept the world for exactly what it is: unfair, mean, graceful, luscious, and magically illogical.

My mother defends, "They don't even know what causes Parkinson's, so how can they know I have it?" She is also magically illogical.

It's been three years since her diagnosis, three years since she first sat at my kitchen table and lost the thread of an easy conversation, her face staring and expressionless, her arm shaking, her eyes that tell two stories narrowing now to none.

———•◦•———

Before my mother moved out of this home and into the mobile home that she and my father chose reluctantly, she had a garage sale. She sold things dear to her for reasons I could not understand. She said, "I got this Hummel for only three dollars. And this original oil painting for twenty." I could not tell if it was the object she loved most or the bargain marked by the object. She sold these things for a significant profit. I'm talking a couple thousand dollars overall.

This weekend she is having another garage sale. It will be at her new home in the mobile home park called "Happy Hills," for seniors only. They're sponsoring the all-tenant sale. She spends weeks getting ready, pricing items, doing nothing less than a stock inventory.

When the day arrives, everything is priced and recorded on a tally sheet. At six in the morning, people start knocking on her door, and she is ready. She steps outside and lifts the plastic wraps from the sale tables, unveiling a masterpiece. You could mistake your shopping experience in my mother's carport for a pleasant day at the local outdoor mall, the way the dresses hang elegantly on the makeshift racks, the way the jewelry is still in its original box, velvet, satin, lush, *ten dol-*

lars, firm, but she'll take five. She misses her days in retail; you can tell by the way she greets each garage-saler individually, cradles each purchase in bubble wrap, places it in a box, and says, "Thank you. Enjoy!"

Inside, my father sits in his La-Z-Boy. He's been sick recently. His kidneys have failed, and his heart pumps like a locomotive just to push a hairline of blood through the dark and narrowing tunnel of his veins. In addition to cleaning, cooking, doing laundry, and shopping, my mother now has to give extra care to my father. Though she's squeamish about needles, she has to administer his insulin shot. She washes sheets that are often bloody due to my father's blood thinners. "I am not a nurse," she says. And my father, a military man to the bone, has devised a ritual around administering his shot. The syringe must rest on the counter before use. The insulin bottle should never touch porcelain. The nurse who taught him how to give this shot mentioned he should insert the needle at a twenty-two-and-a-half-degree angle. His compulsion to "do the right thing" has a military precision to it, and he has translated that twenty-two-degree angle into an absolute that he asks my mother to adhere to without fail. My mother wears tie-dyed scarves, rainbow socks, and Dr. Martens sandals. Neither my mother nor my father is malicious or mean; they are simply as made-for-each-other as Rush Limbaugh and Shirley MacLaine.

My father rises from his chair at ten in the morning and calls my mother in from the sale. "I need to take my shot," he

says. Then he disappears into the bathroom. Moments later, I
go inside to ask my mother how low she will go on her pew-
ter collection. As I enter, I watch her place the hypodermic
needle on the counter. Her body quivers like a tree in a sharp,
undecided wind. "Is that right?" she says, and my father ad-
justs the needle slightly, then nods, yes. He says to her, "Don't
do too much, today, Marge." He says to me, "I worry about
her. She's not well, you know. She needs rest." An hour later
he rises from his La-Z-Boy, pokes his head outside, finds my
mother in the middle of a group of people, collecting money,
socializing, saying, *Thanks, enjoy!* and he says, "Marge, aren't
you going to make lunch?"

Five years ago, before Mom had Parkinson's, my partner and
I took her to Sea Ranch, a quiescent stretch of beauty nestled
in the redwoods along the Sonoma coast. We rented a small
house with an ocean view, and daily we walked through
shaded woods laced with ferns and mossy creeks that meandered, like us, toward the sea. At the base of the steep hill
a collection of boulders demanded we scramble on all fours
to reach the sea. I thought Mom would turn back, but she
laughed when I doubted her agility. She negotiated the tangle
of rocks easily, showing less fear and more grace than I.

At night, as the California sun turned to cool, gray fog,
we made popcorn and hot chocolate and watched old black-

and-white flicks: Bogie and Bacall, Tracy and Hepburn. "It's a shame about Katharine Hepburn," my mother said. "Her Parkinson's."

My mother has always been good at pity. I have not. "I don't think her shaking is from Parkinson's," I said. "Anyway, she handles it well. She still takes part in plays." My mother nodded, her eyebrows growing more asymmetrical as she watched Kate in all her glory.

Last week, we returned to Sea Ranch a second time, a sort of rendezvous to see if what we had gained there the first time—peace of mind, rejuvenation—was still available to us. My mother did not walk down to the ocean on the wooded trail this time; she did not scramble over the rocks, and I did not pity her, but instead, found a new path to the same ocean.

Instead of watching old movies, we lay in front of the picture window and watched the sky turn to night. Twice she saw what she said was a star stuck in a black hole. "See the way it moves so quickly—like a race car bumping up against the edge of that black hole?"

"I don't see it," I told her.

"Yes, look! It's like a black whirlpool, and that crazy star's just frantic, trying to get out, but the black hole just sucks it down."

I looked up. The sky, to me, remained only an endless theory of possibility. The stars were so lush it was difficult to separate one from the other; they blended together and milked the sky with light, only the brightest among them adding texture and points. I never saw the star stuck in the black hole, desperately trying to get out.

When I returned home, I researched, again, the symptoms of Parkinson's. I learned it is more than a tremor, more than a crooked body that cannot easily find a point of balance. It is a smorgasbord of symptoms that, along with its more recognizable traits, includes memory loss, disorientation, and dementia. Hallucinations and schizophrenic behaviors can be side effects of many of the medications used to manage the disease. Like a smorgasbord, however, the person with Parkinson's does not necessarily have all of these symptoms; each symptom exists as a mere possibility.

Throughout the trip, though, my mother saw UFO-like stars trapped in black holes. She listened to foghorns one evening when there were no ships in the bay; she remembered, in detail, things that had never happened, and on occasion, she failed to recall what did take place. On the way back into San Francisco, a city in which she lived for several years, she asked, "Do we have to go over that one bridge?"

While at Sea Ranch, we ventured out into the world of commerce on a few occasions, and my heart ached as my mother searched for souvenirs, trinkets, anything to help her remember the event. But it was more than memory loss that drove her. She shopped here with the same urgency she displayed when buying bargains at home. When we returned from a day at the ocean, she clung to her new sweatshirt the same way she held to her discount at Joslin's, as if her experiences would be lost if not made tangible, as if her discount illustrated, in no uncertain terms, the amount of love she felt for her family and friends—if only she could give them what they were worth, if only she could grasp and hold on to what she was worth. But she could not.

It occurred to me then that in no other time in history and in no other place but America would I have this experience of losing a parent so slowly, so ethereally, so painfully in exactly this manner. In my mother's day, *choice* meant three makes of automobiles (if you had the money), one brand of tennis shoe, two brands of coffee, and marriage at eighteen. Today, the definition of choice would not fit on this page, nor in this volume. Overwhelmed as she is (as we all are) with the ease of fulfilling her external desires, she seems to have mistaken them for her dreams—or perhaps she has simply learned to mistrust what she dreamed.

Suddenly it makes sense to me that my mother wants desperately to get more than she paid for. In what other realm of her life has she ever been given such a break? In what other realm has she ever been marched into an arena and told, "This can be yours, or perhaps you'll choose this."

I fantasize this happening for her now: She is eighteen again, and suddenly she can choose to be married or not; she can choose to have children whenever and if ever she wants; she can walk over to this rack and pick up a college degree, a few "self-improvement" courses, or a selection of art classes; she can go to this display case and decide if this marriage is working out; she can go to counseling if it is not, and if it still does not work, she can choose to make it on her own. At some point in her life, she can choose to live by herself if she wants. She does not have to live under her parents' roof, then under her husband's roof, then under her children's roof, and in her final years she does not have to spend every ounce of spare energy she has caring for her husband, keeping her vows because she is loyal and good, and so is he. I fantasize she is Katharine Hepburn, and in spite of her place in history, her gender, her class, she was able to make choices, and she chose well, and because of choosing well, she can go gently into that good night—or, if she chooses, she can rage against the dying of the light. I fantasize that the black hole has finally released that crazy star.

But this is one of the accomplishments my generation has made: the overwhelming ability to choose. Because I live it, I have never truly recognized it, and recognizing it now, I want only to be able to deny that it was ever otherwise, because we all want to believe, in America, that our fates are cut by chisels we hold in our own hands, that circumstances do not limit, that time and culture do not dictate. But they do. My generation has nothing if not choice. But what void will we feel at our deaths? What easy pill will ease our pain, or slow time enough for us to question who our daughters and sons are, who we are, who our parents were. Though the world itself may end in either a whimper or a bang, an individual's life does not. In America, it ends like a metronome whose ticking we did not hear, at least until the last measure of the song.

I hear my mother's metronome ticking, and I want nothing more than for the music to grow louder, to drown out the easy comforts that quell her desires and overshadow her authentic dreams.

———— ••••• ————

Five days after our return from Sea Ranch, there is a knock on my door. I open it. It's Mom. She's dressed in jeans and T-shirt, and her hat of the day is a ball cap with her short pony tail hanging out the back hole.

"There's a sale at Joslin's," she says. "They've been bought out. This could be the last sale where I'll get my discount."

I know the gravity of this situation. I know what not getting that discount will mean, what it will do to her self-esteem, and silly as I seem to myself, I share her desperation about the loss. I gather my wallet and comb my hair. As I get ready to go, however, I'm suddenly pleased. This "no discount" may offer a time for my mother to discover her worth in something other than dollars and cents. It will open a space, perhaps, for her to see that I would love her and remain by her until death (and beyond) if she gave me only an ugly rock for my birthday. I want to hold up my Liz Claibornes next to the life and good mothering she has given me and say, "Thanks," not for the clothes.

On the way to Joslin's, my mother unfolds, like the village storyteller, the decline in prices she witnessed firsthand (she stopped by the store before she came to my house). "This jacket was on the two-dollar rack. It had been ninety-eight dollars, then it was forty-eight, and then twenty-four. It's a Ralph Lauren, and I got it for two dollars, *plus* my discount, *plus* my VIP. Came to a dollar twelve."

I pat her on the back. "That's great, Mom. It's a great jacket," and as jackets go, it is kind of cool, especially for a buck give or take a few cents.

But my heart is still aching. Her body is still crooked, and her eyes are still hazed with cataracts and wild with desire. What I want to do is pull to the side of the road or get back on the plane and sit in a room with her by the ocean and listen, for hours on end, to her real stories, to the stories she would tell if both her eyebrows could talk, not only the innocent brow, but the one that is arched sharply and does not understand the world, the one that sees something unjust but cannot name it. But my mother, like all mothers, is a one-sided creature. You either get the kind of mom who sugarcoats everything for you, or you get the kind who criticizes the air you breathe. In your little role as the offspring, you do not get the luxury of watching your parents become their own, oddly whole human beings with quirks and jaggedly adorable imperfections. As soon as you no longer depend on them, you blame them, and as soon as you learn that blaming them for who you are or whatever pain you feel is ridiculous because you are just fine the way you are and pain accompanies every ecstasy of life anyway, just at that moment, you wake up and see that your parents have entered into a whole new territory called old age. You cannot go there. You cannot meet them. You cannot enter.

I look at my mom. Her gray hair beneath her cap is a little wild this morning. She can barely reach the gas pedal. Her face, beautiful to me, is also somehow foreign. When did she become old? At what point did the laugh lines around her eyes turn to effort? At what point did her every tomorrow fill itself with question rather than with promise?

Suddenly, and as if lunacy is a common experience for me, I say, "Mom, I have to take you to see the avocets."

"Do they carry avocets? I've never seen avocets in the store."

"No. You've got to turn around. They're not in the mall; they're in a marsh."

"Marsh? I don't know where there's any marsh."

Eventually, I convince her. "We can come back to the store right after we see them. I promise."

She says, "Well, okay. But they have some really good buys in there, and this is the last sale where I will get my discount."

I take over the driver's seat. I drive away from the shopping mall, down the boulevard of strip malls, and onto some back roads that lead to an open space. The marsh is a mile walk on flat terrain, a distance of which I know my mother is capable.

I park the car and get out. Mom remains seated, her eyes creased with worry. "Is it okay to be here?"

"Yes, it's okay. Why wouldn't it be okay?"

"It's so empty. Is this somebody's land? We're not tres-passing, are we?

"No, we're not trespassing, Mom. Let's go."

Cautiously, looking in all directions, she gets out of the car. We enter the trail as if it is foreign terrain, an illicit jour-ney into what has always been possible. In moments we are surrounded with trees, swaying cottonwoods that give voice to the wind. In a window of sky between the green, the bent figure of a great blue heron passes, his movements deliberate, graceful. My mother knows these birds; they hunted on the small pond behind her used-to-be-home. She says, "There's big blue. That *was* big blue, wasn't it? I didn't know he was still here."

"He's still here," I say, and we continue walking. Though the earth is loose and uneven, my mother's gait is fairly steady, her posture almost upright. Meadowlarks sit on mul-lein stalks and sing as we pass. She had forgotten, too, that meadowlarks were so abundant in our neck of the woods. And we see, as well, the quick flight of hundreds of swal-lows, the seemingly labored flight of several magpies, the oc-casional sign of coyotes and foxes, and a brief flash of bright yellow and red of a western tanager. She says, "I've never seen that bird before. It looks tropical. I didn't know we had tropical birds here."

The trees open up to a small lake, and we round the bend and walk toward the marsh. The land is less verdant here, more mucky. She says, "This should be taken care of. This is not very pretty. Don't you want to go back to the lake and see big blue?"

I stop on the dry land, and I point. The marsh is golden, the morning sun still angled on the horizon. "Look."

My mother looks toward the muddied water. Her eyes light on nothing. "I liked it better back there," she says.

I remain standing in one spot. I don't point again; I just watch the six or seven avocets standing steadily on their too-tall legs, their cedar heads and white bodies reflected perfectly in the shallow water that moves like mercury. My mother's body wavers backward and forward at the waist. I had not seen this before in her, but it is there now, and it can be expected to stay. The Parkinson's is filling her body. She looks from the water to me, and glances back toward the prettier lake, clearly put out. Whatever it was about these avocets I wanted her to see was a miscalculation on my part. I start to turn back.

But my mother's body has suddenly stopped swaying. Her brown eyes are somehow clear again, and she is, for the first time in a long time, silent. She says, "They're beautiful, aren't they?"

I nod. She keeps her eyes on the avocets.

"Did we have to pay to get in here?" she asks.

"Mom, you were with me. You remember. Did we have to pay?"

"No," she says. "But I don't know why not."

I take off my jacket and lay it on the ground, then sit down. I know Mom will remind me the ground is dirty and full of fleas, but I do it anyway. A few seconds later, though, she takes off her jacket, her dollar-twelve Ralph Lauren, and covers the ground with it. She sits next to me. I put my arm on her shoulder.

As if delivered on a screen from a slide show, the words to a poem appear in my head. I say the words almost aloud:

> *if I lay down tonight in*
> *this wet field of light*
>
> *would I feel the flesh*
> *of this terrain folding over me—*
> *a seed planted of*
>
> *understanding. would I*
> *feel the losses shrink away*
> *before the hope of*
>
> *what will already*
> *never return haunts me.*

My mother says, "Are you praying?"
I say, "Yes."

When we get back home, she seems to have forgotten about her discount and the last sale at Joslin's. My father is at my house—he came to visit the dogs, as he often does—and my mother starts telling a story, one she has not told him before, about our recent trip to Sea Ranch.

"We went to the lighthouse in Point Arena," she tells him. "It's one of the tallest lighthouses in America, 145 stairs to the top, and I climbed them all."

She remembers this event accurately down to the last detail. "We climbed to the lens, to the part of the tower that sends light out to sea, but to get there, we had to climb these very narrow stairs. They were completely vertical."

Her description is not an exaggeration.

My father says, "You didn't climb them, did you, Marge?"

"Of course I climbed them."

I nudge her. "Tell him the rest of the story, Mom."

She cocks her head, not knowing what else of significance happened. She made it to the top, that's all that matters to her, and so I say, "She made it to the top," and my father smiles and nods.

But what happened after that matters worlds to me. With all the signs at the entrance of the lighthouse that warned about the difficulty of the climb, we never considered that the descent would also be difficult. My mom, who collects lighthouses, whose favorite book is *To the Lighthouse*, who falls asleep with a miniature lighthouse glowing in her window, was so excited about making it to the top of the lighthouse, she neglected to consider coming down. But as we turned away from the circle of unending ocean that surrounded us at the top of the light, she was faced with a narrow channel with no arm-rails and two-inch-wide iron steps that were placed one below the other in a spiral. As she turned and saw the challenge ahead, I could see the fear in her eyes. But she had no choice. She had to balance; she had to descend.

"I'll spot you, Mom," I said, but there was really no way to do that. "You'll have to turn around and climb down backwards."

My mother's eyes froze. "I can't do that," she said, but then she turned around, placed her quivering foot on the first rung, and placed one foot behind the other. Without looking or holding on, she descended.

What she didn't know was that a group of tourists were crowded in the landing, waiting to ascend to the lens. The twenty or so of them watched breathlessly as my mother's tennis-shoe-clad feet dangled and then blindly found their way to the next step, one after the other, no handrail, no light. I was so focused in on her, I didn't notice the crowd, either. But as my mother's two feet finally landed on deck, the crowd broke into cheers. Several people patted her on the back. Others called out, "Good job," and they meant it. Like her, they were caught in the moment. They could feel the tension and fear she overcame with every step. And at the end of it all, they released their breathless doubts about her ability to make it, and they cheered.

My mother smiled and lifted her face toward the sky like a victorious athlete. "You did it," I said.

"Yes," she said. "I did."

"Margie's Discount" update: Stair number 55 in the Point Arena lighthouse now has my mother's name engraved on it. It was a memorial gift to honor Mom given by the then-lighthouse keeper, Rae Radtkey, after she read this essay.

FIGHTING TIME

My body is mostly earth, mostly water and minerals I hold in common with other animals, the domestic dog and the beluga whale, the mountain lion and the sloth. Save for the way I love this life, the strands of days that glisten in my memory, the winglike appendages of seasons (leaf, rain, snow) that catch light and then fall to loss, the lips of my loved one that part so easily to a smile (encompass my heart), the voice of my mother, my memory of the age she once was arcing desperately to somehow comprehend the age she is now, the age she has become in the meantime, and the impending absence that awaits me, her absence (I brush it aside, until); save for the cinnamon sweet smell of a fall evening, the musty scent of grasses moist with the first snow, the days that were once round narrowing to the squint of an eye, the wink of winter closing, the light it creates within its softened darkness, and the way it breaks, eventually, to spring, trembling, as it does, in the wake of its own beauty; save for these things and the way I love them, my body is happy being earth; it can comprehend returning itself to earth, closing its eyes to this place forever just as it comprehends the day-to-day substance of living, that particular celebration that goes on quietly as the night opens and closes and the seasons barrel headlong into one another, creating the sense of roundness that makes us whole. Save for these things and the way I love them, I could go without a fight into the necessary aging, the eventual and permanent silence between us all.

FIGHTING YOUTH

There are certain memories that, over time, become like dreams, not dreams, because of their sheer palpability. You close your eyes, and they play again, the scents and sounds, the mindset you held back then, when you were younger. They are not nostalgia. They cause a certain discomfiture.

There is, for me, the time I was driving home from a week of camping in Moab, Utah. I drove at night to escape the desert's heat, and because I liked driving at night. I liked to watch the rose-colored monoliths, their human forms rising from the desert floor like a congregation of gods.

I passed through Utah in the darkness, and by dawn I was driving through a pastoral valley in Colorado where free roaming black-and-white cows occasionally lit up in my headlights, and the black road glistened beneath their hooves. On either side of the narrow road were small, white houses. Their porch lamps were still glowing and everything was on the verge of morning. When the cows finally meandered from the middle of the road to the shoulder, my Volkswagen Beetle sputtered forward, the engine making the only sound in that quiet break of day.

I was traveling the back roads, so I figured there was little chance of finding the caffeine buzz I wanted so badly. But as I rounded a bend leading out of the small town, a white stucco building appeared. Its walls were deeply cracked, and the screen door waved slowly open and closed, even though the air felt thick and still. The word *café* was hand painted in blocky, red letters that covered the entire side of one wall. Behind the café stood a huge compound of white buildings connected to another compound that was wrapped in gray ducts. A chain-link fence with DANGER, KEEP OUT signs posted on it surrounded the place. Though it was early morning, there were people moving around in there, working, and a sticky-smelling white smoke billowed from the compound's chimneys.

With my legs trembling and bright white circles flashing behind my eyelids whenever I blinked (the effects of all-night driving), I pulled into the dirt lot and walked to the café. When I opened the door, I saw half a dozen men sitting at the counter and a pot of coffee sitting on a warmer. I said, "How much to fill this thermos?" The skinny man behind the counter turned to look at me. The skin on his face was thick and red, heavily scarred. The men at the counter turned toward me in unison. As my eyes ticked down the line of men looking at me, I saw that each one of them had a distinctive mark—a scar, an appendage missing, an ear blooming red and raw from the side of his face. They wore the white uniforms of the people who worked at the complex.

The skinny man pointed to the pot of coffee. "Sit a buck on the counter," he said.

"Thank you," I said, and I filled my thermos, placed a dollar bill on the counter, and left.

It was a time in my life when I thought I would live forever, or when, at least, the thought of dying didn't portend as much loss as it does now. I had yet to understand the human body as the rickety thing it is, the rib cage poised so precariously on top of the finger-thin spine, each rib bending around the vital organs like fingers of a hand folding around jewels (as if a hand could guard the value), and the legs, with their poorly engineered, wobbly knees holding the teetering weight of the torso. At nineteen, I didn't see the way the spine arcs from one pose to the next like the stem of a delicate flower, the body designed, as it is, for beauty rather than durability. My body still felt like a force with unlimited potential. I believed I could drink that coffee, and if it was full of contaminants and toxins (which I believed it probably was) from that odd complex behind the café, so what? My body could fight things off, endlessly. My body was not susceptible. That's what I believed. I had experienced its resilience firsthand.

Confident though I may have pretended, the picture of the men stayed with me, that sacred geometry of the human body altered so grotesquely by, I assumed, some everyday violence that had taken place in that huge plant where they all worked, their need to make a daily wage—something they couldn't fight off. It was my first glimpse into the sheer rudeness of mortality, to see arms and legs so gruesomely altered, to see the calm acceptance on the men's faces.

FIGHTING AGING

This is what is happening in my mother's body and mind today. Deep within her brain is a dark nugget of matter (the substantia nigra). Its job is to create little packets of dopamine and send them out to the basal ganglia, which opens the package, reads the message, and then initiates movement in my mother's body. The chain of command begins with my mother's will to, let's say, bend her legs and take a step. Instead of things going as they should, however, my mother's will lights the fuse that runs to the substantia nigra and looks frantically for that little package of dopamine, which it does not find because that dark place in my mother's brain is dying well before the rest of her body and mind is ready to do so. There's a very sparse amount of dopamine available, and so the spark scavenges what it can and then, dutifully, carries the incomplete message to the basal ganglia. The result is that the leg does not move, or it moves too much, or too fast, or it spasms. In the face of this biology, there's no such thing as "mind over matter" (my repeated motto as a teenager). There is strength of will; there is persistence, but the mind and the body are one—and in the case of my mother, this mended dichotomy is not ideal.

She was seventy-three on the day the doctor first said, "I notice a tremor in your left arm," and began the tests that, a week later, suggested she had Parkinson's. Now, at seventy-eight, she is homebound, her body ravaged with a disease that has twisted her once-delicate spine into something like a thick, gnarled oak. Her arms reach out for me with every step, her upper body bent forward and swaying constantly as if trying to dodge invisible blows, a perpetual movement that ends at her hips, her lower body so rigid her feet have become anvils weighted to the floor, nothing like the roots of a tree (and a fighter is nothing without nimble footwork).

She repeats her mantra to me: "They don't even know what causes Parkinson's. How can they know I have it?" Her reasoning is as illogical as the disease, but the first part of the equation is true. Parkinson's is "idiopathic," the cause, unknown. Certain causes, however, have been ruled out. In "typical" Parkinson's (when the symptoms appear after the age of fifty) genetics are not the cause of the disease. According to an article published in the *Los Angeles Times* (and many other major newspapers in January of 1999), "That leaves environmental chemicals as the culprit for the vast majority of Parkinson's . . . In announcing their results, [scientists] specifically pointed out that the search for causes of Parkinson's should now refocus on environmental chemicals such as fertilizers, pesticides and herbicides."[1]

If you watched me with my mother for a day, the way I comb the hair around her face, the way I stand with my legs balanced on both sides of a bathtub rim and, with my comparatively slight body, lower her into the warm water, joking with her all the way, listening to her laughter, the way she jokes back with me until she sinks into the comfort of the bath, sighs, and I massage her scalp with shampoo, my clothes soaked from chest to ankle, my heart pounding with exertion, sadness, fear, if you saw these things, you would likely not see the rage that informs my every move.

I have pictures of the home where I was born. In one of them, my mother and father are wearing shorts and T-shirts, leaning on snow shovels, and smiling like monkeys at the camera. Their feet are swallowed to the ankle in a fine dust that drifts, graceful as snow, against the rose hedge that borders our newly landscaped, heavily fertilized yard. Behind them, you can see all the way to the front range of the Rocky Mountains. You can see the distinctive outlines of Eldorado Canyon, whose rock walls embrace one-hundred-mile-an-hour winds that blast through the canyon and, at the mouth of it, spread out and rush low across the open plains. As those winds barreled across the open plains back then, they picked up debris and the first layer of recently farmed, heavily pesticided earth, rolling it like a massive carpet until it reached our neighborhood, where it accumulated in drifts against hedges, fences, the sides of our homes. The families there, mine included, ogled the wonder of wind, the speed and power made visible in the mounds of dust we happily shoveled, like snow. The dust brought with it a real social affair. It was a reason for many families to work outside, together.

Between Eldorado Canyon and my childhood home, I cannot recall a housing development or an apartment complex, not a gas station or a Wal-Mart. It was, as I said, mostly farmland, with the occasional interruption of a few stoic industrial chimneys. They stood erect, just below the mountain horizon, rising from a complex of buildings we knew little about—except what my father, a career military man, told us. He said, driving by the complex one day, "This is the place where they make stuff for atomic bombs." He smiled. "Right in our backyard!" He said it with such glee and importance that sometimes, as a child, I was moved to walk out into the endless, open fields behind my house and push my way through curtains of tall grass and cattails until I could see the narrow smokestacks rising, immutable as the mountains behind them. When I was six, I would stand there at attention, believing the mountains and the chimneys were equal in power and beauty.

I was looking at Rocky Flats nuclear weapons facility, ten miles or so upwind from my backyard. The waste from that facility was a part of the dust that rolled across the land and accumulated in our backyards. It was the dust we shoveled so merrily, content and privileged, as we were, to be able to live our day-to-day lives under the splendid Colorado sky.

These are the memories that enter my head as I bathe my mother. I run the sponge down her spine, noting the way the vertebrae bulge distinctly, like a row of garden rocks tucked just underneath her first thin layer of skin, curving this way and that, each curve cupping a mound of spasmed muscle. "I have bones sticking out of my back," my mother says curiously. "It doesn't feel like my spine." She believes the hip replacement she had a few years back has floated to the surface of her body; she can feel the metal protruding, she says. I have not been able to convince her that the bone and metal she feels are her muscles, once supple and strong, made rigid as steel by the disease that inhabits her body.

I've grown to realize that what comes naturally is either this, or that; either the nostalgic images of my mother as a young woman working and playing in my childhood home, or the very vivid picture I see of her now: her body bent, her mind struggling to form words, her face, with the stiffness typical of Parkinson's, trying to smile. I attempt to conjure the mother I knew only two years ago, the one who was aging gracefully, enjoying her elder years, working out at the gym, gardening, swimming with her group of lady friends who were so dedicated that they went to the outdoor pool even during the first snows of winter. On my way to visit my mother at her senior home, I sometimes see that group of ladies with their transistor radio poolside, each of them keeping the beat of the music, singing as they work out. My mother is no longer among them, and I can't get a picture in my mind of her ever being there with them. My memory of that time has become theory.

It is, I think, my brain's way of forcing acceptance, the present bridging to a distant, golden past with nothing in between, no direct access to yesterday or last month.

It happens to me also with land (my body is mostly earth). Though my childhood and the ground I walked then

seem so vivid—the detailed scents of summer, the way birds
flew up in bunches and turned all at once, like a living cloud
exhilarated by sky—I can't recall, in detail, the hills I walked
a year ago, the same hills that now lie beneath the new shopping mall. Though I spent the past five spring seasons watching a pair of mated bald eagles fledge their young in a tree that
stood where the food court is now, I can remember it only
vaguely. The place seems as if it has always been as it is now:
food court for eagle, and my mother's body seems always to
have been crooked.

It is this gap between ideal nostalgia and the present time
that makes loss palatable. I struggle to suture the gap and
restore what I know to be true.

———◦••◦———

I struggle to close the distance, sometimes, even in myself.
Throughout my early adolescence, when I was studying martial arts, I learned that any truly traditional wushu requires a
practitioner to imitate the movements of wild animals. Partially
through that study, I came to feel myself as inextricable from
the natural world. I recall my first teacher's voice repeating to
me a phrase that, these days, has become a cliché: "become
the animal," and now, "become the tennis ball," "become the
guitar"—become that which you seek to master. These days,
people say it mockingly. But the superficiality of pop culture
doesn't change what has been true of Chinese wushu for cen-

turies: There's no way to master a form unless you become not only the animal, but the earth beneath the animal's feet, the elements within which the animal lives—water, metal, air, fire, earth—the seasons, the sounds, the emotions, the parts of your own body related (in Chinese medicine and martial arts) to the essence of that animal. Unless your body becomes inextricable from the earth and all that surrounds it, you can't truly succeed in wushu. You may be a good fighter, or you may move beautifully. But if you practice wushu fully, it creates a weave between you and the natural world that, unlike Penelope's cloth, cannot be done during the day and undone during the night. Though I no longer practice martial arts regularly, wushu was the background of my life from such an early age that it's almost impossible for me to separate myself from the land that surrounds me.

My ability to spar or to do any of the more external aspects of wushu was challenged, however, when I was in my early thirties. In the span of a few years, my body (the same one I believed would live forever) went haywire. My endocrine system, which doctors defined as "the time clock of the body," turned on and off on whim. My adrenal glands worked overtime just to keep me awake, and a cup of coffee caused me to drop into a deep sleep. Language abandoned me intermittently, leaving me for weeks on end struggling even to speak. Though I was only thirty-two, I became postmenopausal within a few months, but at the same time, my body was acting as if it were carrying a child. I was lactating. Doctors were befuddled. The menopause was irreversible, they said. They told me my heart was at risk. They told me my muscle tone would decrease. They warned me of fatigue, loss of memory, and premature osteoporosis. They projected the likelihood of early aging.

In addition to seeking the help of Western, allopathic doctors, I had regular treatments from a doctor of Chinese medicine in San Francisco's Chinatown. The Chinese doctor charged me ten dollars per session, and each session varied from fifteen minutes to over an hour. He held my wrist in his hand, taking the pulses of my qi meridians, then he scrawled some Chinese words on a pad while his wife hand-chopped herbs, weighed them on an ancient scale (the kind of scale used as an emblem of justice), packaged them in large bundles, and handed them to me. They cost me three bucks. When I asked the Chinese doctor what the diagnosis was, he shrugged as if I'd never understand.

But I persisted. "I know a little bit about Chinese medicine," I said. "Can you tell me the Chinese diagnosis?"

As he was taking notes, he said, "The wind enjoys your body." That was it, my diagnosis. The wind enjoys my body.

This was similar to something I had heard before, from my first teacher, too. He'd been raised in China in the forties, and according to him, it was taboo to practice any internal martial art (*nei gong*) in bad weather. It was important to always practice in a warm, well-ventilated place, free of wind, drafts, and extreme dampness. For a man who appeared so tough and demanding of himself and others, this seemed contradictory

to me. Like any teenager, I abhorred hypocrisy. I ignored his
bullshit warnings. I practiced *nei gong* outside in the pouring
rain, "toughening" myself up. If I was teaching a martial arts
class and I had to go from the *kwoon* (Chinese martial arts stu-
dio) to my car, I didn't wear shoes, even if four feet of snow
covered the ground. I liked to face this kind of easy adversity.
My teacher's tender-footed approach to weather puzzled me;
maybe it even pissed me off a little. He bundled up unnecessar-
ily to protect himself from any kind of weather. His weakness
made me cringe.

Although the language barrier between the Chinese doctor and me was even greater than the one I had with my Chinese teacher (the doctor spoke Cantonese, and I had only
learned a bit of Mandarin), I struggled through. "I don't understand why I'm having all these problems," I told him. "I've
practiced *nei gong* for decades. I've done all kinds of things to
keep myself healthy."

The doctor looked at me like I was an idiot. It was clear
my question had pissed him off. "You think you practice *nei
gong* it make you superman?" he said. "The nature world outside is bigger than you are. Out of balance out there, out of
balance in here." He tapped my wrist.

He helped me understand what I *thought* I already knew:
Internal martial arts and acupuncture are designed to balance
and heal the body. In doing so, they also recognize a give-
and-take between the human body and the natural world.
Unlike Western approaches, they are not really designed to

conquer the ailments of the body so much as to return the body to a more "natural" state, whatever that state may be. (Sickness and dying are both natural at some point.)

In my case, allopathic doctors were surprised to the point of fearing a lawsuit (something that never crossed my mind) when after a few months of acupuncture they tested me and declared that my "irreversible menopause" had reversed. This diagnosis came from the result of their own lab tests. My FSH (follicle-stimulating hormone) level went from 100 to 18, the reverse direction FSH levels are supposed to travel during menopause. The reversal was temporary. It lasted only about a year. But that year allowed me the time I needed to accept the huge changes that had previously shocked my body into complete menopause in only a few months.

By this time in my life, I had begun to realize how impossible it was for anyone to "master" traditional Asian martial arts. They are embedded in a culture, and once removed from that culture, they become something altogether different. Like the relationship between the human body and the environment, the products of a culture are intrinsically part of that unique world. Remove them, and you dissect them into unhealthy parts. The American teenager in me wanted to push myself to every physical and mental limit I could imagine. It's a great American fantasy. We see the natural world (and the human body, which is part of the natural world) as something to be conquered. We see a mountain, we want to climb it—or level it, or build houses on it. We, as Americans, believe we can master our physical environment. By combining the rigors of martial arts with the attitudes of my own culture, I had turned my relationship with my body into an SUV commercial. I was splashing through rivers, braving the wind and rain, thumbing my nose at the snow. If my body was in pain, I ignored it; if it was sick, I worked through it; if it was tired, I had a cup of coffee or three.

The particular combination of my own personality traits and the traits of the culture within which I was raised had created a time bomb in my body. But when my endocrine system went haywire, I was forced to accept a balance I thought I'd embraced all along.

The human body is inextricable from its surroundings, and there's far more to the story of one's health than lifestyle and genetics. It's a trick that's been played on us throughout the past few decades. As scientists have found that more and more terminal illnesses and neurological disorders spring from environmental toxins, we have, as individuals, been sold the idea that if we get ill "it is a gift" and we need to learn to interpret how we have "invited" this illness into our lives. Clear up the emotion, eat the right foods, and (we are led to believe) we just might live forever.

There's an arrogance to this "spiritual" approach to illness that seems to escape many people. We—our bodies—are an integral part of a system that is being destroyed from the outside in by the same forces that have sold us the idea that our illnesses are "our gifts." If we can be convinced of that, we will spend our time and money analyzing every minuscule aspect of our diet and lifestyle, which leaves very little time to look at the problem as a whole: the environment is being devastated and we (our bodies) *are* the environment.

I am haunted by the fact that the original name for pesticides was "endocrine interrupters," and that we only began using them after WWII because they were left over from the biological weapons we had invented and used on our enemies. I am pissed off by the fact that popular literature on cancer tends to overlook the World Health Organization's report that states very clearly, "At least 80 percent of all cancer is attributable to environmental influences."[2] In this study, the word *environmental* refers to "everything we interact with or consume that is not freely chosen." It is placed in contrast to *lifestyle*, which refers to "that which we choose to consume: breathing air as opposed to eating dessert, drinking water as opposed to dipping snuff." The martial artist in me wants to be able to fight when I read that "cancer rates continue to rise sharply and a flood of synthetic, hormone-mimicking chemicals continues to exert wide ranging effects on people and wildlife," but I'm uncertain where and who my opponent is.[3]

It no longer surprises me that the girl who was my best friend when I was a child developed, in her early thirties, some of the same "idiopathic," multifaceted symptoms I developed: premature ovarian failure, substantial adrenaline loss, a breakdown of the immune system. We were, by then, living worlds apart from one another, connected only by memories we held dear, and those memories held zero awareness of any subtle, environmental violence combing our bodies.

I worry that when health ailments befall us, we often believe they are either "our fault" or "our fate." But this is part of the imbalance. It is what allows us to push the limits of the land (our bodies) and to overshoot our natural resources (our bodies).

Out of balance out there. Out of balance in here.

It is empowering to believe we can stay in good health by making the right choices in lifestyle. It is equally empowering, however, to realize that these choices also extend to the natural world, the environment. Paying attention to lifestyle and genetics means little unless we also find the strength to fight against the degradation of the environment, to be aware of the imbalances forced upon it, to be sensitive to the balance we are affecting with every choice we make.

FIGHTING INNOCENCE

Three months after I was born, a massive fire struck the Rocky Flats nuclear weapons facility. Firefighters made many attempts to extinguish the blaze with carbon dioxide. The attempts failed. The fire burned through the night. Bits of plutonium, a pyrophoric substance, danced above the mountain horizon like giant sparklers rising through columns of black smoke. Toward the early morning hours, firefighters gave in to an action they had tried to avoid, and some thirteen hours after the fire began, the facility and several hundreds of acres of earth were saturated in water used as a last resort to douse the blaze. Although officials assured the public that any escape of the highly carcinogenic plutonium into the atmosphere was negligible, "there was no reliable equipment operable at the time to monitor the amount of radiation that actually went out the stacks. Not until a week after the fire were working gauges installed. Then, in a single day, emissions registered sixteen thousand times the permissible level—a full fifty years' worth of the allowable quota."[4] No one addressed the contaminated water as it began sinking into the local water table.

This was the first of several major fires at Rocky Flats.

Twenty-odd years after that first fire, I sat on the ground outside the high security fence, listening to Bonnie Raitt, Daniel Ellsberg, Dr. Helen Caldicott, Jackson Browne, and many others. They had gathered on a makeshift stage to draw attention to the plant's dangers. Among other things, they warned that Rocky Flats was the only nuclear weapons facility that had been built in a residential area. In addition to this, records indicated that levels of airborne plutonium were higher at Rocky Flats than in any of fifty other U.S. stations. Dust samples downwind of the plant (where I had lived as a child) showed plutonium concentrations 3,390 times what might be expected from fallout.[5]

What the residents (my family and friends) around Rocky Flats nuclear facility knew was that the plant manufactured "triggers" for nuclear bombs; what we didn't know was that the word *trigger* was a euphemism, conjuring, as it does, the simple metal piece hanging from the grip of a gun. But a *nuclear trigger* is the gut of a bomb, a hockey-puck-sized disk loaded with enough plutonium in and of itself to effect a blast the size of the bomb dropped on Hiroshima. Placed in today's sophisticated weapons, this trigger would effect a blast six hundred times that magnitude. Rocky Flats, the facility in my "backyard," as my father proudly pointed out, manufactured somewhere in the neighborhood of seventy thousand of these nuclear triggers before it closed.

Currently at Rocky Flats,[6] workers are seeking a way to clean up the place and transform this tainted ground into six thousand acres of "hiking trails." Some problems they are facing: to find a way to drain some 4,060 gallons of plutonium solutions from leaky pipes and tanks (they have been leaking into the soil for decades); to locate approximately 1,100 pounds of plutonium that remains *lost* in the ductwork during production (this is enough plutonium to create 150 bombs like the one dropped on Nagasaki); to clean thirteen "infinity" rooms—rooms that, when tested for radiation, cause the instruments to point to "infinity" on the gauge. In the process of accomplishing all this, they must move sixteen thousand pounds of high-grade plutonium through Denver and across the country to South Carolina.[7]

I wonder who will hike the trails when they are completed, if the interpretive signs will tell visitors they are walking only a few feet above infinity.

FIGHTING TIME

As I have been writing this essay, the latter part of fall has been turning to winter. I sit at my desk and look up toward a window that opens to the world. There are times when the light blazes through so harshly that the letters on the screen of my computer disappear in the glare. I keep typing, and as my pupils soak to black, full of light that blinds me, I see, occasionally, the silhouettes of hundreds of Canada geese flying overhead. Their heavy, winged bodies intersect the small window in a geometry of flight that flickers like a candle, its flame nearly out, then surging, the wings of the wild birds, bending, extending. When this happens, I sometimes stop writing and go outside. There is a small parcel of land behind my home. It is not my land, but there has been little else in my life that seems more like something that cannot be taken from me. That place is like a child, I suppose. Others might look at it and believe it was a pitiful, small thing—some fifty acres of tall grass and weeds, a pond, some cattails, and the dusty lunar landscape of a prairie dog village with its mounds and craters. I stand there, and as the Canada geese cross the sky, the sun goes out for a few seconds in the same way it darkens and chills when a heavy cloud passes. The sound of the geese falls around my ears like jazz. I can hear not only their nasal honking, not only the brush of their wings through air, I can also hear the creak of their joints as their wings pump up and down. I allow myself to fall into the sheer stimulation of every one of my senses: my eyes full of flight; my nose full of damp, snow-melted grasses; the wind touching my skin like fingers; my ears selecting the specifics of sound, my voice, a laughter I cannot hold back.

Recently, I have learned a developer wants to turn this land into a plot of convenience stores. Although martial arts have taught me how to walk away from a fight, they have also taught me that sometimes, you can't walk away. For me, now is that time. It's not that I abhor convenience. It's that I feel slathered in it. It no longer feels like a privilege, but like a burden, like something so heavily out of balance that it has invaded me, the body I have sought to care for and whose balance I have finally learned to maintain.

One of my wushu teachers once told me that one goal of martial arts was to learn to embrace the world with all your might, but when the time comes to let it go, to let it go; however, I have never reached this ideal. It still gets under my skin, this world. I want the imperfect grace of it all to pour over me. I want to swoon when I see beauty, to cower when I feel fear, to remain strong enough to allow every emotion to weaken me. I want to wrap myself around these moments, squeeze them for their beauty, their grace, their ugliness, their sorrow.

At night, when I fall asleep, I sometimes imagine the backhoes digging into the fleshy hip of that land. They are superimposed on the image of my mother's ravaged body, bent and torn by a disease whose cause was preventable, but not by her. Although I know the natural world may continue to renew and restore itself without my intervention, the fight I feel in my bones is not only about restoring the natural world. It is about healing myself, my loved ones. Sometimes I feel overwhelmed by the vastness of it all, by a momentum outside my body that seems unfathomable. Then I remember that I know what it takes to fight a good fight. It know that rage must fade away and give itself up to a steady, constant compassion, a focus not on what I choose to fight against, but what I choose to fight for, to cling to, to love. Because sparring, doing forms, meditating, they all share in common the incredible strength it takes to move from one point to the next with as much clarity, integrity, compassion, and unmitigated intention as possible. They have created, in me, the simple ability to stay the course, to know when it is necessary to fight, and when that time comes, to fight with the soft and fluid stillness of a river.

The territory of Rocky Flats Nuclear Weapons Facility became Rocky Flats National Wildlife Refuge in December of 2006. The center of the refuge is fenced off and allows no visitors due to what the DOE has called "long-term surveillance and maintenance." The outer 4,000 acres offer a Federal Wildlife Refuge where people can walk, hike, bike and picnic.

SNAPSHOTS OF MY REDNECK BROTHER, AND OTHER UNDEVELOPED NEGATIVES

We're at the Lone Star Steakhouse & Saloon, which doesn't live up to its romantic, Old West name. It sits smack-dab between Chili's and Applebee's. We do have to walk through two saloon-style doors to enter, and my brother Roy is wearing elk-skin clothes (and a Peterbilt ball cap that sits high on his head), and he's carrying a six-shooter, as he always does, and his wife's wearing an actual bearskin coat. But the restaurant itself is just another generic link on the chain of what the locals call Munchie Lane.

Roy and his wife, Shondra, both order whiskey, baked potatoes, a slab of beef, bloody rare, and a salad. Shondra also orders a bottle of wine.

When the salad comes, Roy picks at the croutons with his fork like a kid picking at peas.

"What's this stale bread on my lettuce?" he says, barely moving his lips and speaking way back in his throat with an accent I dropped and he perfected somewhere between playing tag in the yard of our childhood home and herding sheep in Wyoming for a few seasons. He eats the iceberg lettuce.

Shondra drinks her whiskey and most of the bottle of

wine and, after Roy pays the bill, shoves the near-empty wine bottle into her coat pocket. "We paid for it; we're taking it," she says. Good point. In the parking lot, she sighs and looks up at the stars. "Yeah, I'm gonna go back to the Wienerbagel, take the noodles out, make myself a stiff drink, smoke a bowl, pop a Xanax, and go to bed."

The Wienerbagel is a Winnebago. The noodles are their three dogs in the Winnebago. Shondra is Mormon.

The occasion of Roy and Shondra's returning to Colorado from their home in Utah is my mother's death. The next day, at the memorial viewing, my brother, with elk skin and bolo tie, the ghosted outline of the Peterbilt still on his head, sits stiff-backed in the pew and never stirs. He blinks slowly, breaking his otherwise constant stare. He's always reticent—Shondra does the talking. But today his reticence is ready to shatter. If you brushed by him, or said the wrong thing, he might stand up and punch you once, then sit back down, motionless. You would not come back at him with a punch of your own. Because, I forgot to say, he carries the gun to the funeral, too. Shondra carries a small paper bag of vodka in the bearskin pocket where the wine was last night. It's barely past noon, and already she loves everyone. Her breath burns more aromatic than the incense. She says, "I love you, you know that? I really love you."

In the background, my mother lies in state.

Before the funeral, I had asked the funeral director to play "Kind and Generous," by Natalie Merchant, as the final song. It's an upbeat tune of thanks and honor.

At the service, when the joyous song breaks the somber mood, Shondra stands up, thrusts her pinkie and forefinger into the air, and bellows, "Rock on, Mom!"

That's my brother. That's his wife.

That's me there, sitting next to them in the pew. I'm the raging far-left liberal with a few college degrees and a CV, which my brother, when he speaks of me, proudly, as he always does, calls a CB. I'm against logging (he's a part-time logger); I'm an ex-vegetarian (he used to work part-time in a slaughterhouse); I don't hunt (except with him, which I'll tell you about in a minute); and I'm gay. His wife tells me every chance she gets that she accepts this in me. "I want you to know, you're the same as us, same as any of our friends. In my eyes, y'know what I mean? Y'ain't no different. None. At all. See what I'm saying?"

It was so early in the morning, it was still night. I sat, looking out my apartment window, excited to see my brother for the first time since I'd started college. I noticed the sky, shiny as a black widow's abdomen, stars like little red and gold hourglasses splattered across it; then Roy's headlights bent around the corner. I shouldered my gear and headed out.

I opened the truck door, saw Roy and Shondra behind the Marlboro mist, and climbed into the cab. Roy nodded hello, stepped on the gas, and shoved a bag of donuts my way. I declined. He gave me a look and dunked his donut in the thermos lid of steaming coffee, steering with his knees.

Shondra conked out after saying good morning, and the rattle and hum of her snore was the only sound in the pre-dawn dusk, until Roy nudged her a good one in the ribs.

She bolted awake and elbowed him back. "What the hell?"

"You're snoring!"

"And you're breathing. In and out, in and out, all day long. It gets so monotonous."

They both held a tough gaze for a second, then cracked up laughing. Roy popped a cassette into the deck, and Bob Seger serenaded us up I-70, into the mountains.

When we arrived at the site, Roy and Shondra set up camp. There wasn't a lot of campfire chat. After a round of blank early-morning stares Shondra hitched herself up to a standing position and crawled back into the tent. Roy and I headed out.

We walked together into the woods, our feet sinking soundlessly into beds of soft grayish-blue fir needles. Just as the sun tipped over the bony-backed mountains, we ducked into a copse of aspen trees. In that light, the gold leaves turned bright enough to hurt my eyes, sharp dots of light in the lift-ing fog.

Roy sat with his back against the trunk of a tree. He smiled and patted the ground next to him. I felt like a kid again, like Roy and I were in our old tree fort, and no one else knew it, and *this* was the life.

We didn't say anything for the next four hours. Time passed like time should pass—rich and quiet and all your own. We walked, occasionally. Then we sat. We didn't have to talk to know when to walk and when to sit. It was cold, and the woods smelled nutty and sweet and dusty, the way autumn woods always smell; that's what I noticed. What Roy noticed was the fall leaves rustling in a particular way. Even if I were not his sister, I believe I could have seen his thoughts because he thinks them so hard. His posture changed. His back straightened against the tree he'd been leaning against, and he lowered his eyes. Seconds later, seven does spilled from the aspen into the meadow. I could tell by the smallest shift of his gaze that he was offering me first shot.

In that second I heard the blood rushing through my ears like little rivers, and then the sound poured over and out of me, and the woods throbbed all around me, and I couldn't hear a damn thing except this *whoosh, whoosh, whoosh,* and it made my hands shake just a little, and Roy saw them. That's when he caught my eye; I nodded, consenting. It was not my shot.

The deer grazed. He waited, we waited, oh, I don't know, maybe forty-five minutes. That breathing that Shondra had complained about—it seemed to stop. Roy was perfectly still.

If you're not a hunter, what happened next may disturb you. It disturbs me. Because it was beautiful. I swear it felt for a moment like Roy and I had stepped into the crack between two worlds. For no apparent reason—no difference in sound or movement or mood—the deer stopped grazing. They became as still as Roy. Then there was the shot and the scattering of the deer that ran like seeds might blow across the land, and one doe fell to her knees. Then to her neck. Then to her side.

The click of the gun cocking, the blast, the sound of the doe falling, and the crash of the rest of the herd taking off were all one sound. Time layered, no sequence.

Then we snapped back to this world. It was no longer beautiful. I was watching a living being die. It was ugly, as death is always ugly. And it was mean, and it was hard, and it was bloody, and life wanted to hang on; it always does. We field-dressed the deer, then returned to camp.

———

We were best friends. I was seven years younger than Roy, but the gap never really mattered. We were inseparable.

We lived in a smallish town in central Colorado that was no longer rural, but not yet suburban. When my parents first moved there, the place sat next to open prairie and orchards; soon after, a highway was cut through the drought-scarred land, and it turned our neighborhood from a content little community to a place that longed to be noticed as travelers passed us by. The only prominent structures we could see from our westward-facing window were the distant smokestacks of Rocky Flats.

When our father told us, "They make stuff for bombs there! Atom bombs!" I saw Roy's eyes light with wonder.

We spent most of our days outdoors. Roy had pieced

together a four-wheel-drive '57 Chevy from junkyard parts, and we spent our afternoons ripping through mountains and rivers, thrilled with the power we felt in our bones, the rumble of the engine, the accelerator obeying the slightest tap of the foot, taking us wherever we wanted to go. We had motorcycles, too, also junkyard masterpieces. We took them with us hunting. After the kill, we tore through the woods, the high-pitched *ping-ping-ping* of our two-stroke engines screaming through the peaceful trees, wounding the terrain, polluting like only a two-stroke can.

We, not just he, smoked Marlboros back then. The sting in the lungs felt good, the pleasure of knowing we were playing a part in our destinies. We had a good idea of what disease would get us in the end, and there was power in the fact that we would be the ones to invite it. Power, too, in the way we spoke—fuck grammar and the way we were told to talk. Our mouths formed an accent that was not Southern, not Northeastern, not West Coast, but one a them middle-a-nowhere, redneck ways of talking that had nothing to do with place.

Some days, when we couldn't sneak out a car or motorcycle, we'd walk the land behind our house. Toward Rocky Flats there was a rocky outcropping where we liked to hunt for rattlesnakes. We named this place Skeleton Ridge, not for any bones we'd found there, but for a hard white spine of quartz that ran skinny through the otherwise red Colorado dirt.

We didn't kill rattlesnakes when we saw them. We just watched them, their quickness, their beauty. We sat still, the high-altitude heat needling the bare skin on our arms and necks. On rare occasions, we saw a snake strike a rodent. I say "saw," but there was no real seeing involved. One second we were looking at a lazy snake; the next second, the snake had half a mouse hanging out of its unhinged jaws. Three or four surges of the rattler's slithering body, and the snake had a mouse-shaped Adam's apple and a mouse tail tongue. Then the bulge slowly lost its form.

Like I said, we never saw the strike. The sound of it—a sharp rasp of motion—was a memory by the time the strike registered.

Once, after a day of unsuccessful searching, Roy and I gave up. We found a soft-curved rock and lay back, soaking up sun. It was the last day of summer before Roy entered high school. I'm not sure how long we'd been lying there, holding on to that last sweet tendril of freedom, but I can still hear the sound, the familiar sharp rasp that startled us. Roy and I bolted upright.

After that, the world turned surreal.

There was the yelp of a dog, and as we turned we saw a muscular boxer that had leapt at least five feet into the air. A thick, thrashing rattlesnake dangled from the dog's leg.

I can't tell you what happened in the next split second. One moment, Roy was sitting by my side; the next, he was a skinny slash in the midst of the confusing scene. Before the dog hit the ground, Roy had the tail of the snake in his grasp. Then there was the dreamlike image of the snake's body sailing in midair. Roy had ripped the snake from the dog's leg and flung it a distance away. The rattler hit the ground with a soft thud, red dust flying up around it in an *S*. The dog landed, tried to run, but faltered and fell.

The owners of the boxer, a man and woman, came into view next. The woman curled herself around her dog. The man stood above her, his gun out, pointed at the snake.

"No!" Roy cried. "Don't kill it. Don't hurt it!"

We heard the *boom* of a gunshot, and then everything went still.

Roy saw the snake, its body blown to smithereens, and he burst out crying.

"For Chrissakes, kid," the man said. He rapped Roy on the head with his knuckles. "What are ya? A baby?" He pushed his wife away from the dog, then wrestled the boxer into his arms, saying, "Come on, boy, come on!" He tried to make a tourniquet of the dog's leash. The struggle weakened the animal, and by the time the man was able to lift his dog from the ground, it was dead.

On the way home, Roy hiccupped, holding back his tears. He collapsed to the ground about halfway, held his knees to his chest, and sobbed. I sat with my arms around my older brother, cradling him as he rocked. When he stood up again, he knocked me away with his fist in my stomach.

That was the last time Roy and I hunted for rattlesnakes.

I left home after high school and, through a circuitous route, ended up attending a university. Roy moved to a tent in the mountains. He was married by then, had two kids, and the only way we could stay in touch was if he called me from the pay phone when he went to town to buy groceries.

Our conversations were, well, they weren't conversations. They say Inuits—actually they say Eskimos, but PC language has changed all that—have more than a hundred different words for snow. Roy's *yeah* is kind of the reverse of that. It's one word with a hundred different meanings. Take for instance when I learned about recycling in college. I knew Roy loved the wilderness, and I was excited to share this idea with him. "Yeah," he said, meaning: I'm not washing out any mayonnaise jars and mind your own damn business.

"George W. Bush can barely construct a sentence, bro. I can't believe you like him."

"Yeah." Subtext: One of our presidents talks like me. That's pretty cool.

"Roy, Rush's talk show is not a viable source of news. It's biased, provincial, and retrogressive."

"Yeah." In other words, speak English, sis.

The phone was not really Roy's medium, so one morning I decided to visit him. I parked on the road, then started the trek to his canvas abode in the woods. On the way, I passed his small son and daughter sitting in a claw-foot bathtub, a fire burning under the tub. His son had woken at four to haul the water, build the fire, and take a bath.

I trekked on through the forest and finally found Roy's tent. It was surrounded with guns that looked like semiautomatic rifles set up on tripods. Actually, there were only three—but, to me, when you're speaking of semiautomatic weapons, three constitutes a surrounding. The whole scene planted a deep fear in me. A fear of Roy, of his way of living; a sudden, unshakable fear of the undercurrent of violence in my own growing up.

⸺•⸺

We rarely saw each other after that. I finished college and went on to grad school. Whenever I told stories of Roy to my university buddies, their eyes lit up with interest and wonder, like Roy's eyes had when Dad told us about Rocky Flats and the atom bomb. None of my college friends had ever hunted; that alone made Roy romantically cool in their eyes. They may have been living some version of the American Dream, but Roy was living the American Myth—the one of cowboys and guns, of a lot of action and not a lot of talk.

"I told a friend about you, and he's taken up hunting," I said to Roy once, grappling for some common ground. "There's this trend going on right now. People want to pay their karmic debt for eating meat, and this guy's into it. Cool, huh?"

"Guy wants to hunt he should hunt," said Roy. "Guy wants to pay his karmic debt he should take on a few long shifts at a slaughterhouse."

I only went hunting with Roy that once while I was in college. On that trip, when he offered me the first shot, I realized that I'd already taken my last. I'd traded the power of guns and engines for the power and privilege of education.

I saw him again when I came home for the holidays from my graduate program in Iowa. He greeted me with a hefty punch to my right arm, and I returned the affection with the same slug. He responded by pulling a Saturday night special from his pocket and pointing it at me as we stood in front of the Christmas tree. Our family and guests were preparing dinner in the kitchen, Bing Crosby singing on the stereo.

Roy chuckled, then withdrew the gun. He cradled it in his palm like a pet lizard and said, "I can get you one for Christmas if you want."

I said okay. It's hard to turn down an offer from someone who's just held you at gunpoint. But I never followed through to pick up my present.

The next time I saw him was twenty years later at the Lone Star Steakhouse & Saloon before Mom's memorial. Anticipating that meeting had made me by turns giddy and apprehensive. My friends now were all professionals, a number of them were gay, and all of us were "alternative" in some way or another. When we thought of people like Roy, we also thought of people like Matthew Shepard. I recalled sitting with Roy once as he and his friends laughed about the fact that the cabin of two gay men near where he lived (in his tent) had burned to the ground. "I did that," Roy said, with pride. He was joking. I hope.

After my mother's funeral, Roy came over to my house, which is just down the street from where he and I had grown up. Russian olives had begun to take over my backyard, and Roy always carried a chainsaw in the Wienerbagel.

"Where's Shondra?" I asked.

"Ah, she's got some friends," he said, waving his hand behind him.

I was a little stymied. I'd grown fond of the dynamic between Roy and Shondra. It had been over two decades since I'd talked to my brother alone.

Roy walked through the back gate, studied the tree problem, then reset his Peterbilt cap on his head. "Yeah, we'll get this taken care of right quick."

He walked with a limp now, so off balance and rickety he looked like he might have two wooden legs under his jeans. I watched him make his way to the RV, his long gray biker-braid trailing down his bent spine, and my heart ached. He lifted the heavy Husqvarna, and I called out, "You want some help?"

He gave me his are-you-kidding glance and fired up the chainsaw. In his hands, the saw seemed like a needle and thread. He wheeled it into tight places between branches and trunks and, in minutes, my thorny jungle was leveled and the branches and trunk pieces stacked neatly.

"You want to come inside for some tea?" I asked.

"Tea?"

"Or I've got coffee."

"Yeah."

Roy had never been inside my house. We didn't say much. Occasionally, he stood up and looked at one of the photos of Mom and Dad I had placed on a shelf.

After a while, he said, "Well, sis, I better git."

"Oh, okay," I said.

"Don't wanna keep Shondra waiting."

"Nooo," I said.

Neither one of us moved.

Then virtually out of nowhere, a voice called out, "Yoo-hoo!" I peeked into the living room and saw Ebba Meyers, the woman who'd lived one block over from us when we were growing up, at my door.

Roy leaned across the table and whispered, "Jesus Christ, that's Ebba Meyers."

"Yeah, so?"

"So I'm sure I stole something from her or broke something, or maybe wrecked her car."

"She's carrying flowers, Roy, and a casserole. For Mom."

I'll be damned if Roy did not blush.

Ebba let herself in, and Roy's face broke into this huge toothy grin like the kid I'd grown up with. "How the heck are you," Ebba said to Roy.

"Well, I'm not in prison," he said.

"Lightning strike me now, how'd you break out?" Ebba said. She whacked Roy's chest with the bouquet, then turned to me. "I am so sorry about your mother." The floral weapon turned peaceful when she handed it to me. Then it was right back to Roy. They talked in half sentences with references I couldn't follow and shared news of kids on the block, some of whom were, in fact, in prison.

Ebba's kids had also avoided doing major time, but she'd lost one of her kids in Vietnam, and now she had two grandsons in the military.

"Brady's in Kurdistan. Shane's in some place called Yusifiya," she said. "I don't know where that is. Either one of them."

"Fuck that fucking war," Roy said.

Ebba closed her eyes like she was praying. "I don't know how this country got into this mess."

"Has something to do with who's running it," I said. It came out before I'd had time to think.

Roy and Ebba both shook their heads. It surprised me that they were not staunch Republicans.

"No way. I like some of those guys, yeah. Might be good to hang out with them. But hell if I want someone I'd hang out with running the country."

"God forbid," laughed Ebba.

"C'mon, Roy. Don't tell me you support any politician who supports gun control?"

"I don't give a shit about gun control. I don't own any guns."

I gave him the you-liar look every kid sister occasionally flashes her big brother.

"Not according to the government, I don't."

I smiled. Of course. Making our own rules was part of Roy's and my working-class, Colorado upbringing. We figured the rules were never fairly applied to everyone, so why not conjure up our own code of ethics, our own manners, even our own way of talking.

Roy and Ebba stood shooting the shit a while longer, and eventually I joined in. As we spoke, I felt that old accent working its way across my tongue. Memory quit washing over me; it warshed over me now. It felt good.

By the time Roy and I saw Ebba to the door, night was falling, a chill settling in. We waved to Ebba, then stood side by side on the porch, soaking in the silhouette of the Rockies. Roy said, "All right then, sis," and that was that. He patted my shoulder farewell, and I watched him limp down the sidewalk. It was like a limb of me being sawed off, not a limb I used much anymore, but one I needed anyway, just for balance. I could already feel myself stumbling.

"Hey, bro," I called out.

He looked back.

"Say goodbye to Shondra for me."

"Sure."

"Maybe we'll keep in touch?"

He nodded, then used the side-view mirror to pull himself up into the RV. I watched him light a cigarette, the smoke curling around the bill of his Peterbilt cap. He squinted through the glare of the setting sun and hit the accelerator.

I saw his hand shoot out from the window, waving as he rounded the corner.

THE EVOLUTION OF HUNGER

As their diets changed . . . their teeth, no longer a primary weapon, changed shape, which ultimately led to the development of human speech.

—Reay Tannahill, *Food in History*[1]

We crossed mountains and plains, rivers and deserts, our knuckles raw for dragging them across so many millennia. It was finally time to settle down, maybe plant a little garden, balance our diet of wild mastodon with a few fruits and grains, some leafy vegetables. It was back then when our mouths changed. Our teeth no longer hung like sharp icicles behind our lips. We learned to grind back and forth on our molars. Our tongues became a different muscle, with a different shape, and when we sat down to dinner, new sounds floated out of our mouths—sounds that, with our newly evolved lips, we could recreate over and over. We called the new sounds *syllables*, and as they slid across our tongues, we created *words*. We celebrated our newly found gastrolinguistics as hominids tend to do: with food. Our souls hunger for communication. Our bodies hunger for food.

When I lived in Albuquerque, New Mexico, I hungered for sleep. Depression, the clinical kind, and its best buddy, insomnia, kept me company, and we went walking together, sometimes late at night, or early in the morning: any time, that is, when everyone else was sleeping. Sometimes when we walked, it snowed. It rarely snows in Albuquerque, but when it does, it comes in the night, when you can sip darkness from the sky like wine—a little celebration with confetti. At the first sign of morning, though, the snow sinks back into the earth, soaking the dry desert beneath the city.

I lived on Central Avenue, the skanky end of town, across the street from defunct, boarded-up buildings, strip joints, and neon bars (now closed). The skyline behind the low buildings was humped with dead volcanoes, ancient, impotent, caved in at the crater. But on one particular night, those spent volcanoes looked like tufts of meringue, and snow blanketed the street. The city was like a baby sleeping, and I needed to be quiet so as not to wake it.

I walked alone, unless you counted Ragman as another person, which most people did not. His nickname was given to him by the homed-ones because he had a fondness for suit ties, the kind worn by businessmen. He tied them around his body, his legs, his arms, his waist, his head. Navy blue ties, red ties, Mickey Mouse ties, golf-tee ties, diamond print ties, silk, cotton, polyester ties, all up and down Ragman's body. His skin was leathered, though he was still young; his hair was bleached blond, though his given name was Carlos, and he was skinny as a rock star in his tight, worn-out jeans.

If there could be a rock star of the homeless, Ragman was

it. People in town avoided him, to be sure, but it was 1988, before the paranoia of the masses (or more accurately, of the classes), and we spoke of Ragman with more gravity than disdain. We knew where he had grown up, where his parents lived (in the wealthy, hilly section of town), and the common story was that he had attended the University of New Mexico at one time and, since then, had never really left that part of Albuquerque. It was hard to imagine him as the frat boy who stayed in town, his glory days already long behind him. And so we made him invisible, not because he seemed so Other, but because *there but for the grace of angels*.

So there he was that night, at the far end of the street, walking hand-in-hand with the same depressed insomnia that had snagged me. He danced under the traffic light that went on changing, green to yellow to red, even though there were no cars, just snow reflecting the spectrum back into the night, the street all aglow. This stop-yield-and-go was his light show: He twirled, arms out to the side, face held sky-ward, neckties like ribbons unfurling around him. He didn't dance like a homeless man ghosting the streets. He danced like Carlos, a man with a name.

I watched all that color unfolding from the black-and-white end of the street, in the snow and shadowed buildings. After a while, I walked toward Ragman, and he kept twirling, stumbling, twirling. When I was close enough that he felt my eyes on him, he stopped as if he had never been dancing and walked away from me.

"Hey," I called out. He kept on. I followed. "Hey Ragman. Hey! Carlos!" I'd never spoken to him before, and he had no reason to turn and answer me, except that we were two people on an otherwise empty street at a god-awful time of morning.

He turned. He came ticking toward me with the strange kicking way he walked. He held out his brown-bagged bottle of Mad Dog—the drink the town kids called "wimpy puppy," just to piss Carlos off—and offered some to me. I declined. There was this violent silence between us and a fear that surprised me (mine of him, and his of me). But then, and for some reason I've never understood, that fear vanished like leaves falling all at once from a tree: *swoosh*, the naked branches standing stark. He tilted his head, an invitation for me to follow him. I would never have had the guts to follow him in daylight, but now we walked together through the falling snow.

Ragman was homeless, but everyone knew the place he called home: the couch behind the bookstore, between the Dumpster and the wall. There was a fire pit by his couch, his own little heater, and the police and the bookstore workers ignored the ashes and extinguished the embers if they saw them glowing. We all hunger for warmth.

"Got a smoke?" he asked, as we walked.

I shook my head.

"Tenacity," he said.

"What?"

"Takes tenacity, not smoking. The days just pass. You can't tie your shoes, nothing to look forward to."

"Well, I do, now and then. I smoke. But I never buy a pack."

He looked at me and laughed. "I got that," he said.

I had no idea what time it was, still dark, maybe toward dawn though, because the outline of those volcanoes looked like vellum now, a pinkish, transparent painting pressed against sky.

"C'mon, around here," Carlos said. We walked behind the bookstore to his open-air abode. He sat down on the couch, patted the wretched thing, asking me to have a seat and, homed little snot that I am, I remained standing. Carlos bent over the arm of the couch and brought out a few bulging grocery bags. He pulled out a crinkled-up cigarette, lit it, and inhaled, and rummaged through the grocery bags with his other hand. He took out some slices of bread, a jar of Jif, a handful of little square packets of raspberry Smucker's, and a knife. He slathered the peanut butter on the bread, and I couldn't help staring at his hands—fingernails black, skin like burned wood, his knuckles swirled like knots on pine. Then he handed me the jar and the loaf. "You make your own," he said. "Come on, I won't touch it. Just try it."

How long had it been since this man had dined with anyone? He stood up now and hovered over me, waiting for me to dip my knife into the Jif, and he smiled, an unpracticed smile. I slathered the peanut butter on thick, then I sat down on the soggy couch next to him and tore open a packet of Smucker's. I was frightened, and oddly okay about being that scared.

When I was done, he screwed the lid onto the Jif, then leaned back into the couch. We ate. We smacked our lips. We licked our fingers—you have to when you're eating peanut butter and jelly. Snow fell on us, around us, and the sky faded to daylight. We sat there eating together. Occasionally, Carlos let out a little laugh, like a kid sharing a new toy. "Heh. Heh, heh."

I laughed along with him. "Heh. Heh, heh."

I did my best imitation of Julia Child. *Here we have a sandwich au beurre d'arachide. Oooo, delicious!*

And it was.

> Their wits became sharper and their brains larger as they competed with the lion, hyena and saber-toothed cat that shared their hunting ground.[2]

⸱⸱⸱

After our mouths, the next to evolve were the eyes and heart. It was rough going there for a bit. Some among us still tore at raw meat and used our teeth as weapons, while others of us sat there grinding away, somehow sure we had become more human than the rest. The more evolved among us often gathered into large groups, shared food, and practiced using teeth and tongue to form agreeable sounds, something we came to call *language*. On occasions when our newly found ability to communicate with reason failed us, we ended up being torn to bits by those whose tongues could not yet shape a thought into a word, a word into reason.

This, too, was Ragman's fate.

By then, the snow had quit falling, and the season had turned to summer. Ragman and I had passed each other on the street several times, but that peanut butter sandwich turned out to be nobody's savior. Ragman went to sleep one night, his Mad Dog curled next to him on the sofa. In the encroaching summer heat, some of the young male hominids in town discovered fire. They wanted to see if Ragman would burn. He did.

The city held a ceremony for Ragman. The same people who had crossed the street to avoid him now brought suit ties from home and wrapped them around a tree on campus. Elementary school teachers brought their students. People, kids and adults alike, read poetry they'd composed about this man who looked, in retrospect, like a Maypole—some posthumous happiness in him that we invented to comfort ourselves after his passing. The community came together and made a little chapbook of Ragman tales. They stapled the binding. They sold it and gave the proceeds to a shelter Ragman loathed to stay in, half-wild as he was.

Since I'd never settled with a tribe in New Mexico, I eventually migrated across the country and ended up back in Colorado. I was philopatric in reverse. I had not returned home to birth my own children, but rather, to help those who had birthed me pass on to the next world.

My father met me at the bus station, and we rode together back to the place where I was born. There were the ritual hugs, the kisses, the assessment of my latest hairstyle, my clothes—the general primate grooming that takes place in families. After that, there was food. Homemade bread, brownies, corn on the cob, potato salad, lemonade, baked beans, deviled eggs. "Eat," Mom said, "Eat more," every gesture meant to fill me with all the emotion she felt, but could not say.

My father slapped the bloody flanks of a dead animal on the fire and sweated in the Fourth of July heat. Then, with a floral apron wrapped around his barrel waist, he came smiling to the picnic table and set the meat out for us to devour. What I didn't know, but now suspect that he understood, was that this would be his last Fourth of July, his last summer barbecue with his family, his last night of fireworks and late night conversation with loved ones.

In his younger years, my father was not much of a talker, preferring grunts and occasional outbursts for most of his expression. But evolution takes place even in one lifetime. His tongue grew heavy with all the silence gathering in his mouth. Slowly, he began to tell stories. That evening, he told stories I'd never heard. Forty-some years of silence and still words can rise up from the husk of a man and spill into the world like milk: no crying over them, or the lost time they represent.

He was a man who had never taken a vacation that required flying on an airplane (a drive to the nearby mountains satisfied him). His overseas expeditions were mostly by ship, all part of his life in the military, a life he had never planned to live. He'd tried delivering milk, then selling shoes, then door-to-door vacuums (it was during the era when people opened their abodes to strangers carrying huge suitcases with appliances inside). But none of this work offered the steady income of war, and so, in 1944, he donned the Navy blues and went sailing.

On the sea for several days and nights, his world changed. There was nothing so beautiful, he said, as navigating waters with no land in sight, the cradle of ocean wrapping around him and rocking him like a lullaby. But then, after so many days at sea, the island of Kwajalein came into view, and my father remembered his home, his origins on land. "That island sat there shining green in the gray ocean," he recalled.

As my father described the evidence of life on Kwajalein, one of the major islands in the Kwajalein Atoll, his voice turned foreign, as if a poet were living inside this hunk of a man, this angry flesh.

"It looked so peaceful there," he said. He described a crescent strip of land that rose out of the ocean like the back of a dragon, green scales covering it, thick canopy of trees shimmering with night dew, catching the last rays of the sun, turning red, then orange, then saffron, then finally fading to gray.

"The shallow sandbar around the atoll turned the water raspberry-popsicle blue," he said. (Did I know he had ever eaten a raspberry popsicle?)

He said that on Kwajalein he could see the telltale imprint of human life, the way the palms of the trees cupped in a line, bending to the roads beneath, the wooden roof of a building rising here and there, some geometry within the sway of natural chaos.

"Next morning," he said, "Nothing."

"What?" I asked. "What do you mean?"

"We'd razed it overnight. The island was barren. Not a living thing in sight."

He spent the next few months of his life clearing "the debris."

That night at the picnic table, as my father told his stories, the dew of the Kwajalein trees shone in his eyes. But he just kept on talking, never calling attention to the rivulets trickling down the valleys of his cheeks.

After dinner, I turned on my computer and looked up Kwajalein. YouTube showed videos of the shelling my father was a part of, the aftermath of it, the cleanup. Soldiers walked among dead bodies. They sat with their backs to the woodpiles that were once buildings, their faces young and uncarved and shiny with sweat. They smoked cigarettes on the black-and-white screen. I was grateful I was not seeing this in living color. Any one of those soldiers could have been the man who had raised me: my father, first angry and quiet, and now gentle and old. Things evolve.

As I fell asleep that night, I remembered a story my father had told me of his growing up. He used to tell it over and over again, each time with a smile.

"We lived out on the Great Plains of Colorado. Not the

Colorado you see in the picture postcards," he would say, "but the part that looks like Nebraska because it almost is." When he spoke, I imagined the flatness of the earth, the dry, windblown land, dust devils rising up in swirls now and again, then settling back to earth.

His family worked as ranch hands, sleeping in the barn, eating what was given to them. The charge for the males among the ranch hands was to break horses. There was no whispering involved. Instead, my grandfather and uncle used two-by-fours to beat the horses into submission.

But my father was not about to beat horses. Not when he was five, not when he was ten, or even twenty. He knew this in his bones, he said, from the day he was born. He knew it was wrong. So his brother and father went out beating horses, and my father, who was not allowed in the house during the day (women's work), was tethered to the clothesline out there on the plains.

In the story he told over and again, he'd say, "Oh it was a good time. So much to discover, the insects, the birds, a whole world right there under that clothesline!"

I was young and stupid enough to believe his joy. He said it with a smile, like he said everything else that didn't make sense to me, as if every hardship was a joke. It made me angry. And I hated him for it.

The next December, my father missed our family Christmas celebration. He'd been hospitalized with complications from diabetes. By then, I'd had a few hardships myself. There was a gentleness between us, an understanding. We talked about my life and my life partner, Lisa.

"Your relationship," he said to me from his hospital bed, "I didn't used to get it. I thought it was wrong." He shook his head. "I want you to know I get it now. There's so much love between you."

Three days before he died, when the nurse asked him how many children he had, he held up four fingers to show her, then took it all back and added one more. "Who did you forget?" the nurse asked. He pointed proudly to Lisa.

Somewhere in the time I spent with him as he was dying, his story came full circle, in my view. When I was a teenager, I knew the boy who had been tethered to the clothesline, now a man bursting with anger and unable to express an emotion. As an adult, I came to know the child my father was, the boy who refused to beat horses and grew up to be a man who wept openly for a lost island that was once full of life. The two were one and the same human.

Before he died, my father had one request: to go home and have a big meal. A feast, he called it. He gave me one hundred dollars and said, "Go shopping. Buy food for a feast!" When I tucked the money back into his shirt pocket, he looked at me blankly. "What the hell am I going to do with this where I'm going?" he asked. He shoved the hundred bucks back at me.

So with money as my only weapon, I hunted the aisles of the grocery store and came home with a turkey, yams, cranberries, potatoes, green beans, pumpkins, wine, nuts, fruit, *a feast!* The dinner table looked like an autumn landscape—red, orange, burgundy, deep green—with steam rising from the colors like fog. The house smelled of sage and cinnamon. We—my mother, father, Lisa, my youngest brother and older sister—gathered around the table. Fire glowed at the center, candles flickering in tribute to the now-defunct fire pit.

We clinked glasses, and my father made a toast that has always seemed odd to me: "At least we have this dinner," he said. As if there had been so many things before that had fallen short. As if we had spent most of our lives miscommunicating and fighting about small things. As if somehow our last months together were what mattered, and those months culminated in this single night, this feast.

A few days later, my father took his last breath. Lisa and I were holding his hands when his gravelly lungs sputtered to silence.

Philopatrism: one word evolved from two, *love* and *father*. It had brought me home.

At least we have this dinner.

> *What self-preservation and the quest for food did during millions of years of evolution was to transform a particular family of apes into two-legged super-animals.*[3]

———◦•◦•◦———

Further evolutions confound us to this day. In the world of primates, both bonobos and chimps are so genetically close to us that many scientists contend we probably share the same genus (Homo).[4] But these same scientists are unsure why some Homo sapiens seem to be more closely related to bonobos, while others appear to be part of the chimp lineage. When bonobos greet strangers, for instance, they break the ice with a little sexual healing. When conflict arises, they work it out by making love face-to-face, a rare position in the undomesticated animal kingdom. Among bonobos, same-sex love is even more common than in chimp culture, and females are the center of society.

Chimps, on the other hand, often greet strangers by making war and defending territory. In a conflict, violence is almost inevitable. Same-clan murders occur regularly. Males dominate the social structure, and chimps rarely, if ever, make love face-to-face.

One common denominator found in both bonobo and chimp, however, is the love of food: the social nature of eating, the joy of sharing a simple meal. As omnivores, they forage all day long, munching delectables. But after a particularly successful hunt, they sometimes have a proper sit-down, sharing their meal with a large group.

The winter after my father died, I found myself still in Colorado, walking early mornings through the streets of

my hometown, vaguely hoping for another peanut butter and jelly sandwich, a family feast, something, anything
to fill me. By then, my mother had joined my father, and
both their bodies had turned to dust. As they disintegrated
back to earth, my remaining family exploded like an errant
firework—sparks flying, confusion, embers of memory suspended, and then, complete darkness. In the midst of it all,
my youngest brother (who has a form of autism) became
homeless, and although I had the chance to take him in, I
opted not to. Instead, I found him an apartment and offered
to pay all but fifty dollars of his rent. But this was not his
choice. And so, soft and gentle, intelligent and confused as
he was, he ended up on the streets.

When he did, I began having a recurring dream in which I
had murdered someone. The first scene of the dream showed
me standing before a bloodied body that had been pummeled
beyond recognition. I was the killer. The biggest part of me
wanted to confess, but I could not bear the pain my confes-
sion would cause my partner and those I loved. And so, self-
ishly, I took the body into a muddy swamp and buried it. As
I write this, I can still smell the musty-wet scent of the mud,
can feel the fleshy arms and legs as I wept and shivered and
covered the man I had killed.

Frightening as the dream was, it never woke me from
sleep. Instead, it dropped vivid as a memory into my mind
midday—so vivid that, in midconversation with someone,
my chest would cave, my heart would race, and I would

grope for a place to sit down, literally gasping for air. For a few long minutes, I could not make sense of it. The dream felt as if I had lived it, as if this was some other side of me that had bloomed in the night (the werewolf myth, the dual mind of a serial killer) and somehow I had suppressed it. I thought I should see a psychologist to figure out the meaning of the dream, to make the recurrences stop. But it carried such emotional impact that I worried the psychologist, too, might think I had this shadow side that killed in the night and shrank back into my quiet bed by morning. I pictured myself confessing to some cold case, living the rest of my life incarcerated, convinced I had committed the ultimate crime.

Guilt is very likely an adaptation unique to humans. My guess is, guilt has evolved over time to instill the virtue of uncertainty in the otherwise vastly arrogant two-legged super animals. As the dream recurred, I thought of Carlos, of his family, of what sadnesses and situations had led them to let Carlos go, away from them forever. I imagined them driving by, seeing Ragman on Central Avenue, knowing he slept behind the bookstore where he eventually burned.

I began searching regularly on the Internet for my brother. Nothing. No trace. I wondered what I would do if I found him. Take him a peanut butter sandwich? Sit with him on a musty couch, surrounded by a torn construction-paper skyline of spent volcanoes lit by a saffron sunrise? Knowing that the beauty of predawn light doesn't change a thing, even though it is there, every day, in all its glory?

Yes, I think that's what I'd do. My brother Tack and I would sit and eat, and reminisce a little, maybe talk about our earliest shared memory: when my older brother, the one everyone admired, shot and killed a number of birds in the field behind our home. Tack and I collected the feathered corpses and made coffins for each, and the field transformed into a bumpy graveyard where song had once been. Maybe my brother and I could talk about that. Or about the time when I first realized there may have been something off about my *shy* brother, when a kid down the street threw a football too hard and knocked the wind out of me. Tack, already man-sized in eighth grade, came at the kid, beat him to a pulp, and never showed an emotion. He punched the guy with the same *thump-thump-thump* that came out of him when he watched *Jeopardy!* and recited the answers before any contestant tapped the buzzer. When questioned about why he beat the guy, Tack shrugged: no words.

Here's another thing I remember about Tack. He almost never joined the family for Thanksgiving dinner. Even as a child, he begged to be left out of the gathering. If he did join, he ate fast, then got up and left. As an adult, he claimed to have other things to do (though he didn't date, and he had only one friend, a guy the family had only seen once or twice over the course of a decade, or so). Then one day I found out the truth: that Tack was ditching the family on Thanksgiving to go down to the homeless shelter and serve food. There but for the grace of the angels, and then the angels took flight. I don't know how many years he did this, or when he stopped doing it. I remember seeing, on his dresser, a small stack of letters thanking him for volunteering regularly.

> *The loss of the [wild] chimp and gorilla seems imminent. Moving chimps into the human genus might help us to realize our very great likeness, and therefore treasure more and treat humanely our closest relative.*
>
> —Morris Goodman, *Proceedings of the National Academy of the Sciences*[5]

I strive for the bonobo side of the animal that I am. Being human, I mostly fail. I think of Ragman, of my father, of the people who lived on the island of Kwajalein before my father and his ship arrived. I think of the horses my father refused to beat. I think of my homeless brother as I eat my warm meal in my brick house, and I feel the angels brushing wings with the likes of me, a land animal who wants to believe in flight but is given to fits of gravity. On Thanksgiving, I feel my brother with me, and I know it's a comfort I've devised for my own selfishness. I want to believe that gratefulness can heal me. I want to believe in Thanksgiving, that one day set aside for gratitude can bring people together in our nation.

This is what Sarah Josepha Hale believed in 1863, when her seventeen years of letter writing to the White House finally made a difference and Thanksgiving became a national holiday.[6] It was not the pilgrims bursting the seams of their Puritan penguin suits that gave us Thanksgiving, after all. No, it was Sarah Hale, who hounded first President Buchanan and then President Lincoln, begging them to set aside a day to celebrate "the power of food, women, and home." Hale wasn't the first to suggest such an idea—people had been proposing different versions of the holiday as early as Thomas Jefferson's presidency—but Ms. Hale's vision remained clear, even as Civil War scarred our land. In 1863, at the height of the war between states, President Lincoln finally acquiesced to Hale's specific requests.

And so on the fourth Thursday of every November—originally it was the fourth Tuesday—I sit with my family (no blood relations here, all choices made with the heart) and give thanks. We pass yams and stuffing and turkey, and we celebrate every bite, every dollop, every sip of wine. We laugh and we light candles and we have a feast, because at least we have this dinner, this time together. That evening, I go to bed and feel satiated right down to the pores of my bones. The bed cradles me, and I sleep curled next to the one I love, surrounded on the bed by five animals and so much gratitude.

In the morning I wake to a world that pulses beauty in its sunrise veins, but whose little cells of people seem doomed to repeat rather than evolve. I am among them, the déjà vu of centuries, millennia, the wars of eons, of gods, of islands blasted to barrenness. But the sunrise is still saffron, melting above solid mountains, and the beauty drips from the sky onto the human mess of us all. And after centuries, millennia, eons of eating—of stuffing my privileged self to the gills that I no longer have—I wake hungry, achingly starved to become more human: the beautiful animal in the core of me craving the evolution of it all.

BACK WORDS

would like to be a fool. A raven. A coyote. A man whose body is painted in wide bands of alternating black and white, my face like a zebra's, my body a totem. I would be particularly foolish should I become such a man, because as I sit here today, I am a woman. But fools do things backwards, the lines between man and woman, animal and human, heaven and earth, not so clearly delineated as they are to us, the rational ones whose bodies are all one color.

I would like to be a fool. I would like to wash my hands in dirt, feel the cool, brown earth cleanse me of my sorrows, my pride, my arrogance, and of the belief that cleanliness is next to godliness, when god is most likely dirt, the gritty transformation, my hands like a seed in that solid darkness, like the roots of a tree, all creation beginning beneath this surface. I would like to dry off with water, to be constantly warm in that submersion, the water pressing my body close, a constant fluidity I could not escape, my skin breathing like gills, the substance of life folding around me. I would like to step in the same river once. I would like to learn from water, the way it penetrates without force, the way it wears away all that is solid, stubborn, immutable, the way it understands time, the way rivers tick ahead constantly without praying for immortality, the way they are full at every moment, though we see them rise and fall, the way water connects islands without destroying solitude, the subtle connections between, the silence of water.

I would like to be a fool. I would like to walk backwards, never forward. I would still reach new places, my movement always ahead, but my eyes cast behind me so that I might see where I have been, where I have come from, the troubles that have beset my course of action, the reasons I have had for celebration, for sorrow, for gratitude, my history, the collective history from which I have emerged and which I am still creating. I would like to keep my eyes always on these things because, looking back, there is always something substantial, and looking ahead, there is an emptiness I cannot help but want to fill—but oh, the more richly I might fill it with the knowledge of what has come before. Living in the present is overrated. It is walking with the rhythm of the past in your bones that matters. The fool lives in the past and is forever in the moment, a Zen mistake, a clock without a battery, its hands spread open on either side of noon.

I would like to be a fool. I would like to say hello when I am leaving, goodbye when I am coming. In this manner, I would remember, from the beginning, the potential for loss, and so might learn to treasure before losing; as I bid farewell, I would remember the potential for return, all things circling as they do, into something like fullness, small moments of completion that weave together, like Penelope's cloth, doing and undoing themselves by turns, an unfinished pattern that guides a weary traveler home, as when Athena says to Odysseus, "Keep the unnameable word in your heart," and the man, poor rational hero, remains adrift for yet another decade, trying to speak what could not be spoken—the word in his heart, his home; the journey at hand, his home.

I would like to be a fool, to keep the unnameable word in my heart, to speak in silence, in silence to speak, to move in stillness, to be still in movement, to end at the beginning, to begin at the end.

I would like to be a fool.

RADICAL

AS IN ROOTSY, OF THE EARTH,
DIGGING TO THE ORIGIN,
RESULTING IN CHANGE

LEARNING FEAR

Friday night and the gals and I are driving around, doing nothing but being teenagers. Vicki and Laura are sitting in the front seat, smoking cigarettes; I'm hanging my head out the back window because the ashy-sharp scent burns my nose. My eyes water as the cool, dry wind smacks my eyeballs. Laura's driving. She's sixteen, blond, Italian, pretty. Stevie Wonder's singing, "You are the sunshine of my life," on the radio, and Vicki, the oldest among us, already pregnant at seventeen, is drinking a Pepsi, flicking the ash off her Kool. We're laughing so loudly we can barely hear the music, and then we're suddenly quiet, so quiet there's time enough for me to notice that the layered silhouette of the mountains against the fading blue sky is beautiful, the tenacity of daylight holding on against the darkness that inevitably falls. Laura Deloria and I have known each another since first grade, and although my military family has moved about while hers has remained here in Colorado, I have always considered her my best friend, even during the years when we never spoke. I have little in common with Laura now, other than this, the distant love we share, a recognition of time passed. That's what I'm thinking when a truckload of guys pulls up next to us and Vicki, for no reason, rolls down the window, bats her eyes, and says to the football player closest to her, "Excuse me, sir. Do you suffer from impotence?"

Laura's eyes light like the flash of a camera—everything frozen for that second. The guys in the truck roar, words but none of them comprehensible, all of them obscene, then Laura peels out, tires screeching, back end fishtailing. She runs a red light and cuts off onto Lookout Mountain Road, a steep thing that coils skinny as a whip up the side of a mountain. She and Vicki crack up laughing, but it doesn't seem like laughter to me. They clench their teeth, lips pulled taut, eyelids propped open like puppets, and they're so giddy I can almost see the nerves underneath their skin, feel the electric current pumping through their bodies like hot sparks.

I'm in the back seat, and when Vicki asks her question, I laugh a little bit, too. It's funny, the randomness of it all when you're sixteen and the world won't make sense no matter how you twist it; still, I know Vicki shouldn't have done what she did. When I see headlights bouncing in our rearview mirror, swerving from one side of the narrow, sinuous road to the other, I *really* know she shouldn't have done it.

"Are they following us?" Laura says, incredulously.

Vicki looks back, and their laughter recharges like the sound of an engine downshifting to pick up speed. "Sheeee-it." Their words mock fear, all in fun.

But that changes. We near the top of the mountain, and our 1967 Chevy Nova is too clunky, too fatigued to make this feel anything like the very cool high-speed chase Laura and Vicki are pretending. The car chugs along at thirty-five, fifteen on the horseshoes, and the truck tailgates us, the guys in it quiet now, not leaning out the window, not playing any games.

Laura pulls out a cigarette, touches the end to the red hot coils of the car lighter, inhales. "Shit," she says, a whisper, no mockery this time. Her eyes cast upward to the rearview mirror.

"Are they still there?" Vicki says.

Laura nods, her eyes skittish, from mirror to road to mirror.

We're coming to a scenic overlook with a small parking area. I say, "Stop the car."

"What?" Laura says.

"Pull over, and stop the car."

Vicki turns all the way around in her seat to glare at me. "Fucking crazy." She looks back at Laura. "She thinks she can fucking beat them up."

"I didn't say that."

Laura snorts, because this is what she and Vicki hate about me, that I don't smoke pot or cigarettes, and already I'm teaching a martial arts class at a private high school. They want nothing to do with my goody-goody, health nut, oh-so-philosophical bullshit, and just then, the truck goes from tailgating to bumping us. We feel the slight jolt, enough to steer us off course for a split second, almost enough on this skinny road to send us flying over the edge of the mountain. Water wells in Laura's eyes, but no tears fall. "Fuck," she says.

She pulls over, shifts into neutral, then turns around in her seat and looks at me.

———⋄———

Before going out that night, Laura and I were hanging out at her place by the pool—unheard of in our little cracker box suburb where front yards consist of tufts of grass in dry dirt, the whole area cluttered with Big Wheels, car transmissions, and stacks of old tires. Any day of the week, you can see fathers sitting in lawn chairs under their carports, radios tuned to Broncos highlights. They don't move, other than to sip their iced tea or beer. But Laura's parents are different. They're real partyers; they spend their money on fun, rather than necessity, and as far as most high school kids are concerned, Laura's house is the place to be. Her parents are active in the community—PTA, church barbecues, Sunday evening softball, the Elks Club, and because her mother is the Avon lady, people frequent their house, strangers who become friends because Laura's mother, a woman with dark auburn hair and a Lois Lane body, is sweet and gracious. "Thank you. Come again," she says.

"Thank you, Norma. Thanks for the iced tea, too."

Laura was allowed to smoke in the house. She was allowed to say *bullshit* and *fuck*. She had cool parents.

As we were getting ready to leave for the night, her father joined us out by the pool. He leaned on the cheap umbrella table, sipped his cocktail. It was not his first of the day. He wore a Hawaiian shirt and shorts in an effort to be suave, but with his bony legs and long face, he looked like Pinocchio on a tropical vacation. Laura and I were just getting out of the pool, and she stopped for a minute to talk to him. "Can I use the car tonight?" she said.

"Where you going?"

"Out."

The smart-aleck answer that every teenager gives bothered Laura's father, I could see it in his eyes, but he said nothing. He just turned back and gazed at the pool, lazily, as if he were rich and had all the time in the world. Then slowly, smooth as a Vegas lounge singer, his arm reached out toward Laura and he tucked his first two fingers into the cup of her bra, feeling her breasts. "You need money?" he said.

Laura pulled back and pushed her father's hand away. She said, "Dad." He retreated like a shunned boyfriend who knew he'd get what he wanted in private. He handed her a twenty and the keys. He laughed a little.

The headlights flood the car like an interrogation, then go dark. It's pitch black up here, the stars like holes torn in a blanket of night, the light of heaven shining through, if you believe in heaven. If you don't, it's just a black dome specked with light that is already history, the distance creating a chasm you could never cross. And it is silent.

The guys don't close the doors as they get out, and the beat-up, powder blue Ford looks winged, too heavy to fly. There are four of them, and for a second I wonder how all those guys were crammed into the cab of that truck. Then my mind clicks in; I size them up. One guy is skinny, probably not considered strong, but his arms are long as a monkey's. He's wiry, and I know he's more powerful than he thinks. Another guy is huge, solid as a pit bull, but his legs are skinny and he locks his knees with every step. He's an easy target, and I'm not one to wait. Once, when I answered the phone and heard an obscene phone caller whisper into the receiver, I gave him my address. Then I went out and sat on my front lawn. He never showed. No unfamiliar cars drove by. My mom and dad were angry, but the whispering voice never called again.

These guys, however, are not on the end of the phone line. They laugh as they walk toward us. They swagger, swig their beers, take their time. They're not bent on hurting us, not really. Their pride's been hurt—and they half-believe Vicki's provocative question was a come-on by a bad girl who wanted them to follow her. They might be half-right, but when you're seventeen and pregnant, you don't always know what you want. All these thoughts run through my head in a few seconds, because they're not really thoughts. It's just the way my body responds to fear: assess the danger; find the quickest way to skirt it. And this time, I realize, we *can* skirt it. I look at Laura and say, "Floor it!"

She stutters to say something, but I interrupt.

"Pull a U-ey, then floor it!"

Laura wastes no time. In a minute, we're flying down the road we had crawled up seconds earlier. The guys from the truck scatter like pool balls to get out of our way, and Laura and Vicki find this hilarious. They howl louder than ever.

I sit with my head propped on the back seat between them, peering out the windshield. There's a turnout behind some bushes, and I tell Laura to pull off and cut the lights.

"What the fuck?" Vicki says.

Laura does what I say.

"What the fuck? Fucking stupid. No, Laura, keep going."

When the truckload of guys passes us, Laura laughs, a real laugh this time. Her brown eyes catch mine in the rearview mirror, a kind of thanks that doesn't need words. Vicki turns quiet. We pull out and follow the distant taillights of the Ford down Lookout Mountain, James Taylor singing that sweet lullaby to himself, and no way for any of us to turn around on this tight mountain road.

—◦•◦•◦—

At school Laura and I have become estranged. I carry a paperback in my pocket and read whenever possible—lunch, study hall, mandatory assemblies—and Vicki and Laura make fun of me whenever possible. When they retell the story of what happened Friday night, it goes like this:

Laura picks me up before school, and Vicki and her friend Cindy are already smoking a joint. Cindy hands the stogie to me, obligatorily, and as usual, I decline.

"She's too good for us," Vicki says. "'Bout got us killed the other night."

"What?" Cindy says.

"Thought she was all hot shit with her karate crap. Got us to the top of Lookout Mountain, four guys after us, and she tells Laura to pull over, like she's going to take them on."

Cindy's eyes go wide. "Did you?"

I shake my head no.

"No fuckin' way. She couldn't. Chickened out so we had to speed down the mountain at the last minute."

"What about the guys?"

"They passed us, went on their way."

I haven't known Cindy all my life. She's Vicki's best friend in the way I am Laura's, since first grade. Still, Cindy seems disappointed in me, and it's hard not to let it get under my skin. She drags on her cigarette, closes her eyes, and rests her head on the open window. The wind tangles her long, dark hair.

When we get to school, Laura, Vicki, and Cindy run ahead of me because Adam Dupree, recently voted "Best Hair," is standing at the school entrance, waving to them. I hang back, take my time getting to class. At noon, I'll leave these familiar hallways in order to teach at a private Catholic high school called Marycrest. Already, I'm looking forward to the lunch bell.

I have a picture of Laura and me that was taken in first grade. Our faces beam at the camera, and our blond hair falls in curls around our shoulders in a manner I've seen only on dolls. It's out of place, our hair, because it is perfectly well behaved, and we are anything but. Our eyes squint at the camera, not with fear or to hide from the bright flash, but because our smiles are so wide we can't help but squint. We hold hands and kneel in front of three other kids whose gazes meander to the borders of the photo. Our free hands make fists, not for fighting, but as if we're trying to rein in the excitement that is pulling us gently but firmly through this remarkable life. We look like we should be in a pop-up book, instead of flat on the page. We have that much energy.

The photo is a still shot that embodies, for me, my entire childhood friendship with Laura. From first to third grade, we shared the same classes at school. We did well in our studies, but we talked too much—mostly to each other. During recess, we usually stayed inside, writing, "I will not talk. I will not talk." We shared secrets, made pacts, swore we'd remain forever friends.

When we did make it to recess, we played four-square, a game at which Laura excelled. She was an athletic, competitive kid who, one day, used her hard-earned winnings in four-square to declare that, for a week, Wilfred Yost would be the leader of all games. Wilfred was the school's whipping boy. His clothes were always torn, and he picked his nose with less shame than most of us. But for a week, he was king of the court, by Laura's command. She was well liked, wicked-smart, determined.

When I returned to Colorado in high school, I anticipated my reunion with Laura. We'd go into her bedroom and talk for hours. We'd confess things we wouldn't dream of saying to another person.

The meeting, however, went nothing like I'd dreamed.

We did scream and hug and do all the things girls do when they haven't seen each other for a long time, and we did sit in Laura's bedroom, catching up on old times. But ten minutes into our conversation, her eyes drooped, then meandered, lighting on nothing. We were sitting on the floor, and she twisted around, reached up, and opened the drawer of her nightstand. She pulled out a compact mirror, lines of coke sparkling like the tail of a shooting star. "You want some?"

I shook my head.

She pulled a rolled-up dollar bill from the same drawer, snorted two lines, cleaned the mirror with her finger, and rubbed the dregs along her gums. She shook her head like a woman getting out of a swimming pool, refreshed. "They have good shit in L.A.?" she said. "I heard they have good shit out there."

It wasn't that I had never tried drugs. I'd lived in L.A. in the late sixties, early seventies, when a single concert at the Forum could get you high—no chance of claiming you didn't inhale.

But everything I ever tried made me sick, or lethargic, or just plain stupid. I didn't get the draw, and when I told Laura that, she lost interest again. She looked around the room as I spoke. She fidgeted.

Oddly, as if our childhood pact had been chiseled in stone tablets, we kept seeing each other. A month or so into our awkward, struggling friendship, Laura told me her biggest secret. We were in her room again, and she was smoking a Kool. We had plans to go out that night, but she was dragging her feet. I said, "We don't have to go if you don't want to."

"I want to." She sat in one place.

"We could stay here, hang out by the pool."

"It's my father. He doesn't really want me to go."

"I thought he said it was okay."

"It is okay. He said it was okay. It's just, he makes me sleep with him."

"What?"

"He makes me have sex with him if I want to go out. If I want to drive the car, have friends over, anything." She was speaking in the same tone of voice my other friends used when they said things like, "My dad won't let me go to parties." "My mom won't let me drive." "My parents want me to get all A's." "My father makes me have sex with him"—as if whatever takes place within your own family is the benchmark for what is normal, acceptable, inescapable.

I don't remember how I responded. My memory fades to black when I recall the moment. I remember Laura telling me that Mitsy, Laura's older sister, had gone through the same thing—her father raped her when she asked for permission to do anything; it was the family rule. I learned that Vicki's father sexually abused her, too, and that was one reason Laura and Vicki had become such good friends.

Laura and I didn't go out that night. Instead, I slept over at Laura's. I didn't want to leave her alone. We talked until way past midnight, then she took a small handful of Valium and went to sleep. I lay there awake, wondering how I could be a real friend, someone who could get her out of this situation. When I came up with nothing, I tried to forget about it. But it was like a splinter of glass underneath my skin. I forgot it was there till something touched it. Then the sharp sliver dug in deeper.

After Laura told me, I began to see it more often. Mr. Deloria was shockingly indiscreet, as if he had a right or, sometimes, as if trying to make an example of Laura, daring me to object. He knew I'd studied martial arts, and he found the notion of a woman being able to defend herself inane. "I've got a black belt, too," he'd say. "And I'm not afraid to use it when someone needs it." He eyed Laura.

Things fell apart in the most fascinating ways back then. The day yearbook photos were taken, Adam Dupree, best hair, arrived on campus with a completely shaved head, bald as a Zen monk. Then, after school, he asked me to a party at Laura's. It was unprecedented: I was a geek; he was a star.

Adam and I arrived at Laura's place stylishly late. Her father greeted us at the door and handed us both a beer. Mr. Deloria was popular with the kids, an all-around good guy, a father who would dance with us and not tell us to turn down the volume when Robert Plant sounded like he was spitting pieces of his lungs into the speakers.

To this day, I sometimes wish I'd been raised Catholic. Maybe then I would have known the significance of the St. Christopher medals my friends wore back then, and I would have understood that popular prayer my friends liked so much, the one asking God to grant us the serenity to accept the things we cannot change, the courage to change the things we can, and the wisdom to know the difference. It was a wisdom I did not possess at sixteen.

The party was a big hit. Mr. Deloria had rented a mirrored disco ball and hung it on a cable above the pool. The red, yellow, and green floodlights that normally lit the area like a cheap Hawaiian luau refracted off the ball. Cool. Psychedelic. On the patio, kids danced in front of a strobe light, their silhouettes flickering like disjointed frames of a black-and-white movie. Kids smoked pot, French-kissed each other randomly, no parents to stop them. We drank beer. We cursed like adults. It was a good time.

Adam Dupree was the social magnet, as usual, this time not because of his hair, but because of his lack of it. People asked him if they could touch his head. They took bets on whether or not it was a joke—maybe Adam had donned a skullcap for the day of photos and the whole thing was a fake. I took a back seat to his popularity, and eventually, I slipped inside the house, hoping maybe I could help Mrs. Deloria bring out more pretzels or pizza.

The Deloria house always smelled a little foul to me, a combination of stale cigarette smoke, booze, and a fleet of small dogs (dachshunds?) that Mrs. Deloria raised and sold. Save for the dachshunds, asleep in their crates, the place was empty. A dim, sallow light, like pus, lit the kitchen. On the linoleum table sat several bowls of Fritos, Bugles, sour cream dip, and a pink and white cake. I sat down, away from the crowd, rejuvenating my slender extroverted tendencies before I returned to the party.

I leaned back in my chair, sighed, and closed my eyes. That's when I heard a sound coming from the darkened living room. I tried to tell myself it was the dogs, but I knew before I opened my eyes what was happening. I knew Mr. Deloria had not seen me sitting in the darkness. It was Mr. Deloria, grunting.

I stood up, and I walked toward the living room. There, I saw the silhouette of his skinny body. His back was to me, and Laura was against the wall, her father's body pressed too close to hers.

I froze. I didn't know whether to leave or to confront him. Before I made my decision, Mr. Deloria pushed Laura aside and walked toward me. "You having a good time?" He smiled.

I tried to answer.

He chuckled a little, as if nothing was wrong. "Everybody else is out having a good time."

I stumbled a little and tried to move away. He laughed at my retreat. "Poor thing. Can't get a guy to give you what you need, huh?"

"Dad, come on," Laura said.

He chuckled and headed for the patio. But before he reached the door, he stopped and looked at me. "You need a little—" He grabbed Laura's crotch. "Doesn't she, Laura?" He laughed again, not meanly, but as if he believed Laura was in on the joke and I was the odd person out, the loser goody-goody who didn't see how much fun I could be having.

"You know, you're an asshole," I said.

He cocked his head and smiled, surprised.

Laura looked at me. "It's okay," she said, first to me, then to her dad. "It's okay."

I looked at her dad. "No, you're an asshole. You're a sick fuck." My words surprised me, too, but I couldn't quit saying them.

He laughed again, then he approached me and started to grab my crotch, too. I didn't think; it was reflex. With one hand, I twisted his wrist, and he was forced to stagger back and away from me. It happened in seconds, beyond my will. And then Laura came at me.

"Stop it," she said, pushing me, hard.

Confusion ripped through my body. I imagined myself

going back at him. It's what I wanted to do. I glanced at Laura. She held her arms out to both sides, keeping me from her dad. Then she started screaming. "Get out of the house, get out now, you fucking bitch, leave!"

I looked at Laura for any sign to let me know she'd been faking it, that she was not mad at me, she was mad at her dad. Nothing. Her anger was impenetrable, directed only at me.

I left the party, left Adam without a date, and I walked home. I walked across the open field where Laura and I had played as kids, the place where we had built a secret fort, our refuge every summer until we were nine. In that fort, we had pricked our fingers with needles, pressed our hands together, and swore blood sisters forever. I missed her, the girl I knew then, the friend I came back for.

⸻⊹⸻

The walls of any high school ooze. When you're a kid that age, there's no getting around it. The minute you walk through those double doors, life changes. Maybe you like the person you become inside the high school walls better than the person "on the outside." Perhaps you're a popular jock, or the prom queen. More likely, however, the walls scream your weaknesses, all the ways in which *you* are *different*.

Monday morning, I walked to school (Laura didn't pick me up), and when I entered, the walls oozed my name. Within seconds I learned that Adam Dupree had tried to kiss me at Laura's party, and I had responded by grabbing his balls—not amorously. After assaulting Adam, I had left the party.

I walked from one class to the other, and crowds of kids parted like the Red Sea, everyone keeping a good distance from me. When I saw Adam down the hall, he glared at me, as if he had really tried to kiss me and I had fought him off. Was he was going along with the story to protect Laura, or was he angry at me for leaving without him? Or maybe he thought *I* had made up the story. The power of mass media pales in comparison to the power of high school gossip.

—•—•—•—

When I look back on the incident, it sometimes overwhelms me with remorse. When I reacted to Mr. Deloria, I didn't consider that Laura would have to remain there, at the party. She would have to give her guests an explanation for why she had become so angry at me. When the party was over, she would have to sleep in her bedroom, footsteps away from her father's bedroom. This was in the 1970s. *Incest* was not a household word then, as it is now. No one would have believed Laura's story.

Other times, when I look back, all I feel is satisfaction. I had stood up not only for Laura, but for myself.

I didn't realize that my act would cause a permanent dent in my high school reputation—that it would be perceived as something revolutionary. Somehow, Adam Dupree was not made fun of for having his balls grabbed by a girl. As the story went, I fought him off, not because he was weak, but because I was a freak. I was stronger than I was supposed to be. Adam submitted because I was not really a girl—but could never be elevated to the power of a guy—so I was somewhere in between: a genderless monster. It was not just the case of Laura's father that created my new image. It was that I sometimes walked down streets, or went to a movie *alone*. Occasionally, I stopped and helped someone who was stuck by the side of the road. I acted as if nothing had changed since we were all boys and girls playing four-square on the playground, all equal in power. I had not grown up. I had not learned how to be constantly, subconsciously, submissive and afraid. I was not a woman.

The stand-up comic Elayne Boosler puts it in a nutshell. In her bit, she says, "My boyfriend asked me to meet him down by the pier after the show tonight." She pauses at the audacity of this idea, then continues. "I said, 'Down by the pier? I can't meet you down by the pier! It's dark. I have a dress on. I have my vagina with me.'" The audience roars with laughter. "'Tell you what, tomorrow I'll leave my vagina at home, in my other purse. *Then* I'll meet you down by the pier.'"

It's perfect comedy: an observation of daily life that, when exposed, makes us all a little nervous. So we laugh. After all, it is absurd. A part of a person's body should not be a liability.

But this is what young women learn. The transition from

girlhood to womanhood includes the lingering awareness that you can be raped. True, a boy or girl of any age can be raped. But the chances increase exponentially for women, and it's not just the *chances* that increase, it's the constant consciousness of fear. As a young woman, you learn you cannot, ever again, walk down to the pier, carefree as a child. You cannot leave your vagina at home, in your other purse.

I didn't talk to Laura again until the last month of our senior year. I was walking across "our field," and between our childhood and high school, it had become a baseball diamond, bright green grass crisscrossed with lawn mower marks, the chain-link fence of the backstop cast in a pinkish hue under twilight clouds. I was taking in the sunset in the way you do when you know you'll be leaving a place. I would graduate soon, maybe go to college, and the prospect made the jagged mountains seem a little softer, more forgiving. After a while, I heard voices behind me, the sound suspended in the hollow air.

A few minutes later, I heard footsteps close behind me. I turned. It was Laura. She had split off from a group across the field. She said, "Hi."

I must have written a dissertation in my head—that's how long it took me to say "Hi." I wished she was walking up to me to say "Thanks, things are better now"—as if her situation could be so easily changed. I wished we were both what we had been in that photo of us in first grade, two excited kids, every choice in the world in front of us, nothing we could not choose, so much hope and energy.

"You walking?" she said.

I laughed a little. "Yeah, I'm walking."

"Where you going?"

"Home."

Her face was red. She struggled to ignore the people behind us. "You want to walk home with me?" she said.

I didn't need any words. I just stopped, turned around, and started walking toward her place.

Whatever we said to each other in the fifteen minutes or so it took us to get to her house was inconsequential. An occasional, "How you been?" A nod. Some laughter that was anything but.

A few doors from her house, she stopped. She said, "You staying in this town after you graduate?"

I shrugged. "Don't know yet. You?"

"Got a job." She smiled. "Hundred bucks a week. Got an apartment. I'm moving out."

I wanted to hug her. I said, "Good. That's really good."

Then, for no reason, she reached out and touched my shoulder. It was an awkward gesture that held within it all our attempts to hold on to the way we believed things should be, the affection we once shared and wanted to continue to share, the expectations we had when we were kids, our excitement about growing up, and the realities that growing up had brought to us. She said, "Take care, will you?"

"Sure. You do the same."

She walked away before I did. I watched her turn the corner toward her house.

———

I don't know for sure what was going on that day in the field. I heard stories about it—that Laura (who had gotten a reputation for sleeping around) had slapped a boy in the face when he grabbed her breasts.

"She's fucking crazy. What did she expect?" people said. "She asked for it, she got it."

When they asked me about it, I ignored them. When the twelfth person of the day asked me, I said, "You know, Laura Deloria could kick your ass in four-square."

The guy looked at me like I was crazy, because I was. I would not succumb, and in the end, I knew Laura would not succumb. I had seen it in her when she was a child. Whatever had happened that day in the field, it was clear to me that she had stood up for herself. She *was* fucking crazy. And good for her.

"I got a job. I got an apartment," she said. Because he did not win. Her life up till then should have been different. It wasn't. But it would be.

"She could kick your ass in four-square." I was downright,

happily, self-confidently crazy. I· was a girl in high school, and although I did not assume I would always win, I knew I always had a fighting chance.

GOT TAPE?

'm standing in my driveway on a spit-freezing cold morning, waving my mittened hand to a friend who has declined
to join me. "No one in this neighborhood's going to listen to
you," she yells through the fog.

I shrug. "I'll be back by dark." And I step into the frothy
jaws of the suburban winter. Within a few strides I'm standing by a mailbox I see every day but have tried to ignore. It's
candy-apple purple with red flames swooshing back toward
the house—the kind of design you see on hot rods. Parked
on the lawn beside a stack of worn tires is a Chevy truck
draped with bumper stickers: I AM THE NRA, RUSH IS RIGHT, and
so on. My friend's voice rings in my ears. Just then, I see some
movement to my left.

"You think he looks good here?" a woman asks.

The man to whom she is speaking ponders the life-sized
Rudolph at the head of Santa's sleigh. He sets his baby Jesus
down on top of Santa's gift bag to help secure Rudolph's ties.

"Excuse me," I call out toward Santa. "Do you know
about the plans to build a SuperTarget and Kmart?"

They look at me through the haze.

"On the land behind our houses . . . the old apple orchards
and ponds?"

"Asshole!" the guy says.

About now I'm thinking of hot cocoa, fireplaces, and moving to another city.

The man walks toward me. "I met that asshole. He's tryin' a sell us a bag a bullshit."

"I . . . I have some letters, a petition against it."

He drops Rudolph cold. I hold out my pen, jittery with thanks. "If you could both sign, and maybe jot a note in your own words, make it more individual."

I hear the pen scratching, then he shoves the clipboard in my direction. "Westminster is OUR town," he's written, underlining it about ten times.

His note hits the nail on the head. In order to Target our neighborhood, this developer must override the Comprehensive Land Use Plan—the single document created by city officials and residents in concert. It states that this land should never be used for retail. I'm out here going door-to-door because I believe the collective voice of the citizens should not be silenced by a nonresident whose annual income trumps ours by a few million.

"What're you gonna do with them papers?" the man asks.

"Deliver them to city council. Maybe organize a group."

"You name the place and time, we'll be there." He shakes my hand. I wave goodbye through the maze of lights and plastic figurines and run back home.

"It's great. You should come along," I beg my friend.

"They signed?"

"And volunteered!"

My excitement gets to her, and she joins me.

Next house. A stout man wearing perma-seamed slacks, white shirt, necktie. If it weren't for his slippers, I'd think he was on his way to work. I smile. "Morning! You heard about the plans for the SuperTarget?"

"No."

"On the land where the ponds are." I position the clip-board so it will slide easily into his hand.

"I don't care," he says. And he shuts the door.

My friend goes home to her hot cocoa. When I return that evening, though, she flips through the letters, surprised. "You got all these signed?"

I nod. "And this is the list of volunteers."

———

Up to this time, my only attempt at civic duty had been to attend a few "COG" (Community Organized Government) meetings. At my first COG, five people attended, three of them city employees. My fellow attendee was mainly concerned about how he could keep kids from setting his fence posts on fire.

At the next COG it was just the city volunteer coordinator and me. She had a projector, and we watched a movie about the problem of Canada geese in the area. I learned some nifty tips about how to keep them from defecating willy-nilly on my lawn.

Recalling these vibrant evenings, I feared my list of volunteers might be so many empty promises. Against my better judgment, I rented a conference room, capacity 300, in a hotel. My workouts that week consisted of running from door to door, delivering fliers that announced the gathering.

I arrived that night just before it was time to start. It was not a bad showing: about twenty-five people, sitting at great distances from one another. I introduced myself and began. People trickled in as I spoke. They trickled and trickled. Thirty minutes later there was standing room only.

I was nervous and excited. "We need a volunteer for community actions leader, someone who can set up eye-catching booths, stuff like that," I said.

A hand shot up. "Me and the missus could do that," said Silas, the fellow with the holiday lawn display.

The momentum continued. I ticked down the list of task forces needed—legal research, fundraising, media relations, city relations, planning liaison, et cetera.—and soon we had ten task-force leaders and a dozen or so people on each team. At the end of the meeting, we brainstormed and planned for our first organizational meeting.

For several days afterward, I tried to figure out why so many people had shown up that evening. There was no precedent for it. Our neck of the woods is known locally as outletville. The indoor mall brims with ninety-nine-cent stores, wholesale clubs, and those new "security" stores that sell mace, brass knuckles, and a variety of small knives. People here are generally working toward moving out of the area, not coming together.

It's true I'm out of place here—probably the only person who fleetingly considered actually voting Nader/LaDuke—but everyone else is out of place, too. There's scarcely a common thread between us, except this: We're buffered from endless strip malls and a twenty-four-plex theater by the 108-acre tract of land that is now at risk. Deer, herons, bald eagles, ibis, and fox live here. The property hooks up circuitously with miles of open country, a narrow paradise gasping beneath the wide Colorado sky, snaking all the way up to the Rocky Mountains. Aside from its beauty, this land offers the only occasion I've ever had to talk to my neighbors. People walk their dogs there. They fish in the ponds. Silas stables his horse at the old pony farm that will be condemned if this project is allowed to go through.

In any other situation, the leaders who came that night—a gay couple, a former Black Panther who is now a Republican, two college kids, a Hmong couple, a Libertarian, a born-again Christian, and a handful of liberal-leaning Democrats—would never have gathered under one roof. If diversity's what it's all about, then our neighborhood is all that and a bag of chips. But without a shared sense of purpose, diversity spells conflict and isolation, not opportunity. I figure that tract of land is what brought us together. None of us is about to give that up.

The group agrees to meet after the holidays. In the interim we're all supposed to do a little research. My job is to sign us up for a city council meeting. That's easy. We have a name now: WATCHH: Westminster Alliance To Conserve Home and Habitat, so I make one phone call to sign up WATCHH for the city council meeting, and I'm done. I e-mail the group and ask them to prepare. My e-mail, however, crosses with an incoming note from the city clerk. "I'm sorry. We have to delete you from the agenda." Furthermore, the note says, "No one from your group will be allowed, under any circumstances, to address your elected officials concerning this matter."

What?

This lights a fire under our melting pot. "It's unconstitutional," says Silas.

"Gag order," says John, the former Black Panther. But after several meetings with the city attorney, we feel powerless. The city is within the law. In Colorado, if there's a public land dispute between two "groups" (in this case, the developer's corporation and our grassroots group), the case becomes a trial and the city councilors become judges. If a judge hears "testimony" a priori, that testimony (i.e., the voice of our group) will be thrown out. Furthermore, if we wish to hold public meetings, we must, by law, invite the developer. Otherwise we'll have an "ex parte" meeting, which—you guessed it—turns us mute at the public hearing.

I take this as my first occasion to contact the press. "Sure, that's the law, but most city councils don't opt to employ it," says the reporter. Off the bat, our city is playing hardball.

———•◦•◦•———

Our first official meeting as an organization takes place at my house, and we learn some other sobering facts. "The average amount of retail in most cities is twenty-five square feet per person," says Donna. "You know what it is here? Fifty-three square feet per person. Lucky us. We have an extra two-car garage's worth of shopping opportunities for every man, woman, and child."

Silas's findings add more. He flips through paperwork, then reads aloud, "Better'n 17 percent a them stores stand empty. Look at this chart. We been on a steady decline in retail success since 1998."

"How can the city think we need more new stores?" asks Celia.

Sadly, we all know the answer. Cities east of the Mississippi have a much better chance at fending off excess commercial development than we do because, in general, eastern cities gain their greatest revenue from property taxes. In the West, it's retail taxes that hum the number. City officials are bound to respond more favorably to commercial developers who actually bring in revenue than to citizens who drop very little cash into city coffers.

We also learn that keeping a grassroots group together

takes a lot of work. It's pretty easy to sign a piece of paper saying we all oppose the development. But it's another matter for people who have never had reason to talk to one another to sit together in one room and focus on a common goal. A typical meeting goes like this: Cherry has recently resigned from her job because her colleagues were "too abrupt" with her. One of them, she says, actually said to her, "Shut up!"

"I mean, I don't have to take that, do I?"

Everyone shakes their heads, no.

"I'm divorced. I have two kids."

"You did the right thing."

I place my hand on Cherry's hand and smile. "Okay. Do you think we should tape the fliers to the doors, or just tuck them?"

"Because, that woman, my coworker, she had it out for me. I'm good at what I do. I'm a good worker. Aren't I?"

"Yes."

She pauses. I begin to speak.

"And I'm bringing up two boys. I'm divorced. Bringing them up alone."

Oh, no, I missed again. The others are tremendously patient. "Yes," the whole group says, in harmony.

"Because, you know, he doesn't give them tough love and I do, and they don't like it much, but it's better, don't you think it's better?"

"Oh, yes. Tough love," someone replies.

Cherry pauses again. I know I have to speak, speak now, say something, anything, except "Shut up!" which is oh-so-perched on my taste buds, but I swallow it and say, "Do you think we should use tape?"

Cherry looks lost. She takes a deep breath as if to talk again, and John jumps right in. "Tape, yes, good. Tape!"

One issue down. How many to go?

The meetings go on like this, month after month. While discovering our strengths, we learn everyone's foibles. We find that Celia is detail oriented, and—good for her—she can take notes and do research. But occasionally, she asks things like, "Where will we put the letters?"

"What's that?"

"The letters to city council. Should they go right or left of the fliers on the table?"

I'm quick to respond. "Either."

"Or maybe behind?"

"No," Donna says. "Not behind. They'll be harder to reach."

"They'll have to reach over the fliers?" I ask.

"Yes," says Donna.

Celia relaxes visibly.

Rita, on the other hand, comes to meeting after meeting and barely breathes a sentence. She's our accountant, does a great job, and keeps her conversations to the financial report. But soon, she finds her forum. Within a few weeks, we're all getting weekly e-mail updates on her health, her husband's health, the health of the dog, who is incontinent, but has medication to control the problem. Her notes trigger an electronic deluge of e-mails about divorce and tough love and dinner recipes.

I try to keep the group on track, but I feel awkward—even intimidated. I don't fit. I don't have a day job or a motorized vehicle, and I am by nature introverted. Each week I give a little pep talk: "We just have to hang in there, folks. We'll win this thing. We will." As I speak, I'm wondering what I've done with the letters I collected last week—did I deliver them, or are they waterlogged in the pocket of my raincoat—and the petitions? I can't recall, and, oh my, is there anyone out there who's good at keeping things organized?

From my lips to God's ears.

"Look, I don't mind being the big fat bitch of the group . . ." This was Renee's self-introduction at our third meeting. "If it gets the job done, so be it." Renee owns a successful ad agency and, ironically, was instrumental in developing the Omni Hotel, one of the most controversial commercial sites along Colorado's Front Range. "Sound hypocritical?" she asked. "Well, that project was consistent with the Land Use Plan. I'm not against development. I'm against silencing citizens' voices."

A few weeks later, Kate joined. Kate had, of all things, a flip chart and the facilitation skills to use it. After a few weeks with Kate and chart, tough love and recipes were distant echoes.

The following meeting, Kate arrived with a box of sample T-shirts and news that a local company had cut us a deal for a custom design. At the same time we learned that Wild Oats and REI had agreed to let us set up booths in their stores. Indeed, we were becoming a real community force, even without breathing a word to city council.

After a few press interviews a reporter said, off record, "You know, the developer hates you guys. I mean, he actually used the word *hate*." I smiled. *Hate's* a strong word, and it gave us strength. We celebrated every attack as a coup. The press we received incited others citizens to contact us. Soon we had a venture capitalist and pro bono attorney working with us. Our constituency grew. Our recognition snowballed.

Still, it was no open-and-shut case. While the elected officials who would determine the "case" were not supposed to have ex parte conversations with the developer, there was no way to monitor that. When John's Motown band played at the local Rotary Club, for instance, he watched the developer and several city councilors twist and turn on the dance floor together. Meanwhile, we sat at our monthly meetings eating finger sandwiches and imagining how slick the developer's presentation would be at the hearing and how feeble ours might seem in comparison.

That's when the obvious became clear: If we were really going to make a difference, we had to quit fighting *against* something and begin fighting *for* something. If you build it, they will come. And if it's a strip mall you build, well, they'll come to that. But if it's a place that incites pride and involvement in your community, they'll also come to that. We envisioned a nature and cultural center, maybe a historical orchard—something to encourage people to stay here, rather than using our town as a stepping-stone to someplace else.

Kate and Renee had organized a good bit of fundraising— local garage sales that contributed profits, a bird walk on the land for a small donation, some straightforward requests for contributions. Renee and I had created a paid-subscription newsletter. Through these efforts, we'd garnered some revenue. "So, let's hire an architect," I said.

Shortly after the newspaper reported our plans, we received a phone call from the landowner's attorney. He said the landowner had been following our work in the news and was interested in meeting with us.

The call threw us into fear. We'd been told by opponents that we were stepping on the landowner's rights, that if his profits were diminished by our efforts, he could sue us. Our attorney assured us this was not possible and offered to accompany us to the meeting. "Too aggressive," Kate said. "We'll bring you in later if there's a need."

⚬━⬩━⚬

The day of the meeting arrives. Renee drives. We pull onto the dirt road and travel through walnut groves and cottonwoods, past grazing horses and stables. A man with gray hair almost down to his waist greets us at the fence, introduces himself as Oliver. He's smoking a filterless Camel. "Reason I brought you here today," he says, and just then a small plane flies overhead, propeller slapping the air. Oliver looks up. "Christ, I had my fill a helicopters in 'Nam, right. Can't stand that sound, right."

He ducks into the house, and we follow. The place is empty. No furniture, curtains, lamps, rugs—nothing. Greasy pizza boxes are scattered like lily pads that we must step over on the way to Oliver's room: a cubicle with a sleeping bag and computer. Along the top of the monitor are a dozen or so stickers of endangered wildlife. Peregrine, otter, whale. Along the bottom are stickers of atomic bombs in various stages of detonation.

"So, anyway," Oliver continues, but then stops abruptly. Across the street from the property sits a miniature golf course. In it, there's a volcano that spews real fire when someone scores. As we speak, a kid lands a hole-in-one, the volcano roars, and Oliver takes cover. He doesn't dive to the ground or anything, but a stormy look brims in his eyes and he hunches over. "To put that thing there—it's an insult to the men who fought for this country. Sounds like mortar fire, right. Nights I wake up sweating, right."

Oliver hops from one subject to the next without shifting gears or turning on the blinker, from Vietnam to childhood in a puff of smoke. "Yeah, me and my best buddy Henry, we built that thing way back when."

"The volcano?"

I follow his line of sight, and my eyes light on a tree house nestled in a tangle of branches.

"Still there," he says.

He stares for a while, then exhales. "You know, homeless people could set up camp on this land, right." No blinker, new topic. "Got nothin' against 'em. Got homeless buddies, right. But if they come here and start cookin' Top Ramen on Coleman stoves, well, it's a fire hazard." He drops his cigarette onto the plywood floor and crushes it out with his boot. "Yeh, I'm the past of this land. You guys're the future." The volcano blows again. Oliver's eyes glaze.

——•◦•◦•——

On the drive home, I'm convinced that Oliver was siding with us.

"Oh, right," says Renee. "He's going to nix the retail deal and donate his land." I consider it. He's got the long hair, the Woodstock gaze. Renee and Kate laugh and laugh. They help me see that Oliver is just one more quirky character in our cast of players. I guess I have a bit of a Woodstock gaze myself.

For the next few weeks, our group is a mess. We're nervous about whatever it was Oliver wanted from us, and there's a new topic on the table. The city has plans to house a sex offenders' rehab center nearby. Folks are up in arms.

"We need to move on. Let them build the damn Target."

"You want to quit now?"

"This sex offenders thing's more important."

"Look, nobody wants a sex offenders' rehab in their backyard, but they have to be built somewhere," says Billy, one half of the gay couple.

"Well, to those of us who have families . . ." says John.

"You suggesting I don't have a family?"

"Oh, don't hit me with your liberal bullshit. You guys are immoral."

"Immoral? You're the closed-minded bigot, but we're immoral?"

I would love to say that just then, the phone rang and the director of open space acquisitions said, "Hey, Oliver's donating a portion of land, and we're hoping to buy the rest, with your help." But that would be implausible.

Except, it's what happened. Okay, she didn't call during that meeting, but the rest is true. Just when we'd sunk to name-calling, the city was ready to work with us on our terms.

A week later we trudge over to Celia's. There are apologies, but most people agree it's time to quit. We've won the biggest battle.

Then Rita, who rarely speaks, says, "I can't believe we've come this far just to turn our power over to the city." She says it softly, and for a moment, it stuns us all silent.

"Well," says Renee, eventually, "I'll put out another newsletter."

"I'll contact the architect," says Celia.

An energy slowly fills the room. I can't help but smile.

Before I stepped out of my house that cold morning three years ago, I might have told you "community" was some kind of Up with People fantasy—like-minded folks sharing a Norman Rockwell moment. Now I think community has little to do with like minds. It has to do with very differently minded people finding a way to get along because we all live in, are connected to, and share a sense of place.

When I hear the coyotes howl at night, all the people in this room hear the same thing. Maybe one of us is making dinner, the other one just rising to go to the graveyard shift. At the same time in our different lives, we stop; we listen. We feel the migrations of birds that pass through here, see the coming of summer on the wings of swallows, and ready ourselves for winter when the herons depart and the bald eagles return. In these moments, a sense of community crashes through our suburban walls.

If I tried to say what made our mongrel group a success, I couldn't pinpoint any one thing. It was as if we were working together to create one sculpture so big that, as we were working, we couldn't see it for what it was. One person chiseled here, another chiseled there until, one day, we stepped back and saw something beginning to take form: our own community. There was no unveiling, no ceremony. But each tap of the sculptor's mallet—the support of a business, the help of an attorney, some economic research—helped shape our little corner of the world into something we intended.

Working together like this, we won our fight against unnecessary development. Now we have to work toward forming the community center we want in its place. In the process, we'll learn even more about one another, and maybe dislike each other more, which means our fondness will also grow. It's November, and as we leave our meeting, Silas starts soliciting help to set up his next Christmas display.

"That's some hideous shit, man," says John.

"You were the one who reported us for light pollution?"

"That's right."

"I always liked those wiseacres who showed up with myrrh at a baby shower," says Renee.

"Well that's just disrespectful," says Silas.

"So what time you want us to be there?" asks John.

Silas ponders. "About ten o'clock?"

Yeah, we'll be there.

"Got Tape" update: Shortly after WATCHH thought the Open Space deal was sealed, it fell through. The landowners decided to hold out for retail real estate prices. But WATCHH was successful in keeping the zoning to residential, not retail. A year or so later, the landowners sold to a housing developer. One or two model homes were built, and then the national housing crisis hit. The developer went bankrupt. To this day, nearly a decade after our efforts, the land sits rela-

tively undeveloped. Coyotes still howl there, and the owls we used to listen to still raise owlets in late winter, early spring. Special thanks to Renee Rinehart and Kate Hyatt for cofounding WATCHH with me.

THIS LITTLE PIGGY
STAYED HOME

Back when my father was living, he was very against organic foods and all "that hippie shit they stand for." When he visited my house in late summer, though, he would often reach into the fruit basket on my kitchen table and bite into an organic tomato. Immediately, he got a misty look in his eyes. "These aren't like those grocery tomatoes," he told me. Those tomatoes were like Proust's madeleine, to my father. The taste turned him from a reticent man to a man who told detailed stories of summer days he spent on the Colorado High Plains, working the fields. "I'd eat tomatoes like apples, straight off the vine, half the bushel gone by the time I got back inside. Oh, I caught hell for that!" he said, smiling, licking tomato juice from his lips.

He picked tomato after tomato from the basket, and I watched the law-abiding man I was raised with transform into a young boy walking through fields, disobeying his parents because he just couldn't help himself—the tomatoes tasted *that* good.

My father was a military man; in his assessment, I was a hippie. I protested the same wars he believed in. We were often at odds, which is why I treasured those tomatoes; they were one of the few things that kept my father and me connected.

The man who planted these magic tomatoes is Jerry Monroe, the third-generation owner of the oldest organic farm in Colorado, the farm to which I belong as a member of Community Supported Agriculture (CSA). CSA is a concept founded in Japan by a group of women who shared concerns about increases in food imports, weakening of local economy, the health dangers of pesticides, and the loss of local, independent farmlands. Rather than butt heads with big business, they worked together to form a direct relationship between farmers and individual buyers who sought healthy, locally grown food. This relationship, called *teikei* in Japanese, translates as "putting the farmers' face on the food," an appropriate title for an arrangement created to celebrate that increasingly scarce natural resource, the independent farmer. By way of Europe, the concept of *teikei* migrated to the United States, landing in 1985 at Indian Line Farm, Massachusetts, where it was dubbed CSA.[1]

Like my father, I'm a realistic sort. I don't think it would be fun to work on a farm; I think it would be hard work, too hard for my gym-developed muscles to handle. I am, however, a fierce advocate of CSAs and local produce. I don't know exactly how I got this way. When I joined my local CSA, my motives were not rooted in political ideology. I had no intention of changing the world, undercutting corporate power, "subverting the dominant paradigm," strengthening my local economy, or aiding the fight against hunger (all of which are direct benefits of CSAs and supporting local farmers). My intentions when I joined the Monroe Farm were downright selfish. I was tired of grocery shopping. The whole scene got me down. I could go to a natural foods store; I could go to Safeway; I could go to the local hippie co-op. It was all the same. Piles of food stared at me like bodies whose souls had vacated them. I was haunted by the way the red peppers curved at the waist, stretching toward one another longingly, by the way the bananas clung to each other and the Napa cabbage lay so quietly in its frilly bed while its blue-collar cousin, the purple cabbage, sat boldly on the edge of the shelf, ready to topple and take off like a bowling ball if someone passed by too abruptly.

Okay. Maybe there was some projection on my part, but the food looked empty to me. After all, most of it had traveled an average of fifteen hundred miles away from its home before reaching that shelf. I was raised a military brat; I commiserated with the "fresh" corn and its lonesome cross-country journey.

My grocery shopping woes were compounded by signs I saw plastered on telephone poles and streetlights in the parking lots: LOSE 40 POUNDS IN 40 DAYS. GUARANTEED! My father was active in three wars: WWII, Korea, and Vietnam. It bothered me that he had fought, as he said, "for the freedom of this country," and that this was part of what we were doing with this hard-won "freedom": creating and marketing food for its *lack* of content, while people in other nations starved. What else, I wondered, were we touting for its lack of content?

As I entered the door of the grocery store, I had only a vague idea of where my "fresh, organic" produce had been. An incomprehensible machine in, I don't know, Iowa, or maybe California, had methodically stabbed the seeds into the ground, and a computer-programmed pivot had watered the seeds until they began to grow. They grew very big, very fast because they were designed by engineers to grow big and fast. Then whatever it was—let's say a red pepper—was plucked from the vine and put to its first major test: Was it big enough? Did it have the right red pepper shape? Did it successfully hide all signs of ever being subjected to weather or greedy insects? Indeed, my shiny pepper passed the test! Proudly, my pepper was then herded into a truck with many other peppers that looked *just like it*. After that, a tarp was thrown over the whole crowd, and together they made the big trip across America (passing many local farms on the way), where they were unloaded into a distributing warehouse, then loaded into another truck and carried to another warehouse, and so on and so forth, until my "fresh, organic" red pepper arrived in the store in Colorado, where it sat in the stock room for days. After a while, it was slapped with a price tag, then displayed under bright interrogation lights. No wonder it looked naked and scared as I fingered through and plucked my prized capsicum from the bunch. By the time I purchased my succulent red pepper, I was at least the fourth person to pay for it. How many times it had been fondled before it became mine is anyone's guess.

Since joining the CSA, however, my relationship with

food has become more trusting, more intimate. On Thursday mornings, the Monroe farm truck backs into my suburban driveway. Jacquie Monroe, blond hair, jeans and T-shirt, hops out, followed by her two kids, Alaina and Kyle. We chat, *What's been going on in your life, not much, how about yours*, things like that, then we commence with the work at hand. Jacquie stands in the bed of the truck and peels the canvas back from the produce, and my nose, nay, my *pores*, are filled with the scent of fresh garlic and onions and broccoli and cauliflower and beans and lettuce and, *oh, I swoon*. I'm ten feet from the truck when this culinary bouquet saturates me, and it occurs to me that I've never smelled *any*thing like this in *any* grocery store. I don't have to press my nose to the cantaloupes in Jacquie's truck to see if they're fresh. I can smell them from ten feet away, the sweet scent permeating the air like—like what? Like fresh, just-picked-this-morning, bright orange-meaty, extra juicy, can't-help-but-eat-it-now *cantaloupes*.

By the time my produce makes it to my driveway, I know *exactly* where it has been. Jerry planted the seeds that were either handed down through three generations of farming on the same land in LaSalle, Colorado, or purchased new from catalogs, not Monsanto. Jerry, Jacquie, Alaina, and Kyle watered the seeds. One of the CSA working-members picked the produce, divvied up the harvest into potato sacks, and loaded the sacks onto the truck.

By the time I haul the gunnysack into my kitchen, huge chunks of loamy earth fall on the floor, reminding me that what I eat depends on just that—large chunks of undeveloped earth. The onions and garlic I get from the farm are not round balls; they have long green tops, great for soup stock, and the garlic is waxy, the skin nothing like the dry parchment I once thought encased all garlic. When I pull the bulb apart to extract a clove, garlic juice drips out. I had to look at my members' newsletter to identify an oddly shaped golden mound as cauliflower. I learned later that commercial farmers hide the florets of their cauliflower from sunlight to assure a uniform color (white), and that the golden color of my cauliflower assures me more nutrients absorbed from the sun.

Granted, the food I get from the farm often looks sallow, splotchy, and ill formed. That's what I love about it. My produce is renegade! It is so lusciously, succulently, and nutritiously *ugly*. The beets are like a kid's rock collection, different sizes and shapes, some round and plump as a heart, others as long as carrots. Some potatoes are like skipping stones, others like large river rocks. Inconvenient for cooking? Maybe. But compare that to this inconvenience: Much of this food would have been tossed into the trash bin if Jerry and Jacquie had continued selling to the natural food stores in the area. According to Jerry, only certain sizes, shapes, and colors meet the "high standards" demanded by grocers. They do not test for nutrients, up to half of which are lost seventy-two hours after a piece of produce is picked, organic or not. They do not test for toxicity. They test for uniformity of size and color. Diversity does not make a beautiful display, and a beautiful display is what opens the floodgates to the insatiable urge to buy. Food in America is often not about hunger.

Jerry also tells me that about 25 percent of all commercial produce in America is thrown away in the field because it is blemished, scarred, crooked, or off-color. Another 25 percent is then tossed during the grading process, which bends to the whims of food fashion. For eons, Grade C and smaller potatoes were tossed into Dumpsters due to their inadequate size. Recently, however, someone noticed that Grade C taters are downright delicious—more delicious even than expensive Grade As. Thus, the birth of a trend; when you order "new potatoes" on the menu at your favorite gourmet restaurant, you are eating yesterday's trash and paying more for it.

Americans, by and large, select their food based on the unwieldy, abstract notion of physical beauty. It's as if we were scoping the produce for a one-night stand, when what our bodies really need from food is a healthy, long-term relationship.

It may be true that you don't know what you've got till it's gone; however, I think there's a more slippery version of the same truth: You don't know what you've lost till you find it.

When my father walked into my house and picked up an organic tomato from my fruit basket, I watched a whole world return to him. Through this food, we celebrated our connection.

PLATE TECTONICS AND OTHER UNDERGROUND THEORIES OF LOSS

EARTHQUAKES

I lived in a small cabin nestled in a redwood forest above the Pacific Ocean. Every morning, I woke up before dawn and counted my reasons for living: the trees, the scent of the ocean through the redwoods, the refracting light that looked liked diamonds on the distant waves, the sound of seals barking at night, my body, the complexity of my body among the billions of bodies together in this world, the way my body could move and my mind could make choices, the way these images and sensations wove themselves into my dreaming, the night air, the morning air, the air.

I recited these reasons like prayers. I hung on to them with all my might precisely because my grasp on them had been weakened. I clung to my reasons for living so I would not, that day, decide to take my own life. But the part of me that believed these reasons for living shrunk to something imperceptible as the day narrowed into working and interacting with colleagues. By the end of every day I was convinced I had outlived every reason I had for living. This was not the romantic depression I had occasionally posed for in earlier days, the depression of an overly philosophical artiste living in an imperfect world. This was different. I didn't choose it; it chose me.

In his essay "The Myth of Sisyphus," Albert Camus says the only serious philosophical question is suicide. But at this point in my life, suicide was not really a question; it did not exist in the realm of ideas. It inhabited my body, my bones, my spirit. It was the only thing that made sense.

Then, one evening, I was lying on the couch, tired from my workday, and a rumbling entered my body like loud music with too much bass. I went to my front door, but couldn't grasp the handle. The door swung open on its own, and I stood in the threshold, watching my truck catapult toward my house. I heard a blast, and then another. The giant redwoods quivered like aspens.

It seemed as if it took me several minutes to comprehend that the earth beneath my feet was shaking, but the Loma Prieta earthquake spanned only fifteen seconds. To this day, I can account for what took place during every one of those seconds. The earth was alive, its body shuddering through the soles of my feet.

My house was damaged, but did not fall down then. It fell two days later, during an aftershock. I was away at the time, and when I returned home, yellow security tape outlined the circumference of the shattered foundation. That night, I slept in a parking lot with other folks whose homes had been destroyed. We gathered around a bonfire and ate food given to us by the local grocer.

I'd been depressed for well over a year when the earthquake hit and had not been able to summon the time or motivation to look for professional help. The hopelessness and lethargy inhabiting my body made that bleak world seem as if it was the only place available to me, and at the time, it was. But something unnamable happened during the quake. For the first time in years, I felt a small amount of hope, and so I began looking for a therapist.

Each therapist I visited cited the grand display of the earth's power as the cause of my depression (they, too, had experienced the incredible quake). They diagnosed me with PTSD (posttraumatic stress disorder) and other acronyms that tied my depression to the losses the earthquake brought about in my life. But the acronyms did little to help my state of mind, and though I generally respect the process of therapy, talking for an hour a week in an air-conditioned office at that time in my life only magnified the disconnection that was haunting me.

I know now that the earthquake was not the cause of my depression; I was already depressed by the time the earth rattled beneath my feet and tore all my earthly possessions to smithereens. But my therapists were right about the quake playing an active role in what I was feeling. It was the main reason I was eventually healed.

TREMORS BEFORE THE QUAKE

To say when my depression began is a little like trying to determine the sneeze that turned the cold to pneumonia, the tremor that triggered the quake. I began to feel, in myself, a crevasse. It shifted viscerally, noticeably; it gaped wide enough to trap small emotions; it began to fill with a deep sense of loss.

At intervals I couldn't determine or control, bits of memory lit up in my mind like scenes from a poorly lit movie. Their dimness didn't frustrate me, but rather, drew me in. I looked harder to see them, certain that their plots were essential to understanding my life. There were the nights I had gone swimming with friends in the local reservoir. They were beautiful for their simplicity, for the clothes we didn't wear, for the way the cool water felt on our naked bodies; there was a silence behind every whispered laughter, and the stars shivered in a darkened sky we normally ignored.

There was the day I went hunting with a friend who had always condemned grocery store vegetarians (like me) who felt virtuous in the "safe distance they kept from the guts of living." She challenged me and my open mind to try hunting again (I'd tried it a few times with my brother when I was younger), to go with her.

A week later we sat silently, alert, almost perfectly still in the woods buried behind our little city. I couldn't recall when I had sat so still for so long in one spot, the world folding in on me in that particular way: light cascading through trees,

my senses heightened to every sound, every brush of movement magnified. It was as if my survival depended on my
utter attention to the world in which I lived.

That night we dined together on rabbit. Though it was
not the first time I'd eaten meat, it was the first time I had
witnessed the relentless beauty and the necessary violence
that eventually became my little dinner; I had seen and felt
the exact moment when the rabbit turned from subject to
object, the warmth of its body in my hands, the earth and its
remaining wildness becoming a part of my body.

Though no single event felt like a cause or a genesis of
my depression, my mind constellated images that carried a
visual significance beyond language. These images relayed to
me exactly how distant my daily existence had grown from
everything most essential to me; they teased me with the
possibility of a real connection to something substantial, not
ephemeral—a sense of history, of my own place within history, of my own delicate but beautiful threads in a tapestry I
could never fully comprehend.

It was not a trauma that caused my deepening sorrow. It
was the recognition of beauty, and of my increasing distance
from it.

AFTERSHOCKS

When the quake hit, I felt the earth beneath my feet, and I
saw the accouterments of my life falling away. In the months

that followed, I no longer had access to many of the things I had relied on as part of my self-definition. I wasn't allowed to enter the area where the rubble, my rubble, lay at the bottom of a ravine. I wasn't allowed to attempt to recover anything. A sign warned me that walking out to that dark ridge was not only dangerous, but illegal. The yellow tape, however, was less than a brick wall, and so one day, I ducked under it, sat on the hillside, and looked down. There it was: my life. A little pile of stuff that I recognized as I might an old friend; I was glad to see it, but I understood that we had to part ways. Most of the things I saw poking through the dirt held memories. I saw the arms of my jean-shirt reaching out of the mud, the pants that I usually wore with that shirt twisted, half-buried behind it. The outfit looked as if it had tried to swim to the surface, as if it had struggled to survive. I saw photo albums and tried to recall the images they held. I saw books I had lugged with me from state to state while I was a student, the books I just could not let go, their spines severed, their muddied pages rigid in the wind, like flocks of dying birds. If I could have climbed down there I would have held them for a moment, then tossed them like doves into the air. From the perspective of the hillside, my life looked so small and so inextricable from the earth. I didn't feel particularly bereft. I felt amazed.

My therapists were surprised by my response. They worried I was on a dead-end path, that perhaps I was leaning toward a romantic desire to drop out of society completely.

They urged me to maintain a realistic balance. The life toward which I was traveling, they feared, was a simplicity conjured by nostalgia.

I explained I didn't want to "return to nature" or to some nonexistent utopian era. I believed then as I do now that nostalgia pieces together the past into an incomplete picture, a lie. I didn't want to go back; I wanted to stop. When I was on the freeway, forced to travel at seventy miles per hour in order to stay in the flow of traffic, I wanted to stop. When I was rushing from one professional meeting to the next, completely unaware of any sight, sound, beauty, or ugliness, I wanted to stop. I did not want a promotion, did not want a cell phone, did not want to trade my house in for a tent, did not want to wear buckskin clothes; I did not want to go forward or back to anything. I wanted to stop where I was, where we are, right now. I thought, *There is nothing else I need*. But the world kept on. I could not stop it. So I wanted to stop what I could—my life, my contributions to a world in which I did not believe. It felt like an answer.

I began to see death as similar to the laundry: I knew it was a necessity of life, and procrastinating it only made things pile up. That's the sense I had—things were piling up—not unresolved emotions or guilt, as therapists and friends assumed, but material things. Houses, cars, insurance, bicycles, kayaks, clothes, photos, computers, software, memberships to gyms, memberships to professional associations, memberships to clubs, knickknacks, books, more cars, more insurance, more clothes. These were the things I had worked for. These were the things I did not want.

SUBDUCTION

sub-duc-tion: when two lithospheric plates collide and one is forced under the other.

The Loma Prieta earthquake was the shaking that upset the 1989 World Series, the quake that tumbled the Bay Bridge, killed sixty-three people, injured more than three thousand, shifted sidewalks by ten feet or more, and made many seaside farmers' neat rows of garlic line up with rows of Brussels sprouts, the cabbage line up with artichokes. The magnitude of the quake was huge; it extended throughout the entire San Francisco Bay area. News reporters called it a "natural disaster"; others called it an "act of God."

My therapists and I worked on "the appropriate response to grief," the digging up of subterranean emotions. But I felt no real excavation. It was just language. What I understood as loss—my job, my nice car, my participation in a world with which I did not agree—my therapists saw as gain, and what they saw as loss—the fact that my clothes, my sofa, my TV, my desk, my computer had gone scuttling down a deep ravine—I saw as gain.

I thought of Saint Francis, the patron saint of San Francisco, who, in the thirteenth century, stripped off all his clothes, handed them to his wealthy father, then began walking a rugged path toward the walled city of Gubbio. Some time earlier, he had heard what he believed was the voice of God saying, "My house is falling into ruin. Go and repair it for me." Maybe the earth shook beneath Saint Francis's feet that day; maybe he did not lose everything, but simply let it go. Maybe his response was not grief, but ecstasy. In Gubbio, he lived with weather and wilderness, celebrating all the elements that decorated "God's house." The beauty and the destruction, the violence and grace.

When I mentioned this to the therapists, they said, "PTSD includes a diminished interest in social activities, feelings of detachment, and the sense of a foreshortened future."

I didn't fear that my life would be foreshortened (wouldn't a foreshortened future be irrelevant to a suicidal person?). I did feel detached. I was sitting in a room, paying an hourly rate to effect the human intimacy that escaped me as I ran from one meeting agenda to the next, saying hello to scores of people I saw daily and whose names I wracked my brain to remember. I knew these folks only in the context of the four walls that surrounded us, like I knew my therapists. Everything felt packaged; I felt packaged.

My therapists assured me that such "external" stimuli were probably not the root cause of my depression. They said, "Let's talk about your family."

I soon felt myself drowning in self-absorbed trivia. I grew more depressed by the weekly search for the childhood trauma that the quake had dredged from my unconscious. But if that was the case, I had no hope of catching up. As soon as I overcame the psychological damage caused by the way I was brought into the world, I'd have to overcome the damage caused by the way I was treated in first grade by some anonymous kid, and the way my first boss treated me, and the way my self-esteem was doused by the end of that job or that relationship, and so on and so forth ad infinitum until I die.

None of my therapists agreed with my suggestion that I could be stuck in depression because I was overwhelmed and felt "powerless over" whatever it was that had led us here, to a place and time where our lives happen almost exclusively inside temperature-controlled rooms sheltered from the pleasures of weather and wilderness. It did not fit into the therapeutic process that I could be deeply troubled by something not born of my ego.

But when I felt the earth rumbling through the soles of my feet, I felt a power I could not comprehend, a wonderful, terrifying sense of awe that had been dampened by living in an overexplained world. When the quake hit, I felt connected to something many would call divine. To me it was the simple mystery of being wholly and inescapably human.

DANCING ON THE EPICENTER

After the earthquake, that constant tug I had felt earlier finally carved its way to my surface, and I was opened like sky. The dark ridge of loss that had been building within me crumbled, and in the rumbling that ensued, I was able to sort things out. I began to live as if my survival depended on my utter attention to the world in which I lived—to the loss, the violence, the absurdity, the celebration, and the beauty.

Outwardly, my life changed very little as my depression waned. I did not hearken back to that indelible hunting trip, buy a shotgun, and take up hunting. I did not become a vegan. I did not sneak "environmentalism" onto the agendas of those interminable meetings I attended. I did not seek to speak more openly about my emotions, or greet everyone I met with hugs. I performed the same tasks as before, but the avenues I took to them were different. I no longer drove to work, but rode my bike. I taught my classes wearing bike shorts and a hairdo that was obviously shaped by a helmet.

On the way home, I usually detoured off the pavement and pedaled through the woods. The path I rode through that almost-wilderness took me right along the fault line that had released its tension in 1989. I could sometimes see, with my bare eyes, the earth moving there: one wall meshing against the other, like two bodies grinding slowly on a dance floor. I gathered my geologist friends to confirm my sighting, and we sat for hours, staring at the wonder of the living earth beneath our feet.

It was not the only time I sat for hours staring at the wonder. The redwoods filled me with awe. The ferns filled me with awe. A deer turd filled me with awe. I didn't wear this awe on my sleeve or market it to others; rather, I tucked it away in a quiet part of me. I was deeply content. On this last point, my therapists and I finally agreed, so I bid them farewell and thanked them for our time together. They had, after all, done me a good turn. Whether or not we agreed about the roots of my depression, they had listened to my arguments (maybe they, too, were frustrated that "distance from beauty" did not appear as a valid diagnosis in the *DSM-III*—the textbook that outlines diagnoses required by health insurance companies). They honored my choice to battle through my depression without the help of medication, which, they said, could have alleviated some of the physical and mental suffering I endured. Eventually, they even nodded to my suggestion that something other than the vacuum of my own ego might have contributed to my depression, but they never comprehended exactly why and how I believed the earthquake had played such a positive role in my recovery.

———

Though the earthquake had instigated the process, other factors had also helped me along the way. Among them was a silent conversation with a poet, Joe Bolton, who, at the age of twenty-eight, a month before his critically acclaimed poetry collection was published, killed himself. On a crumpled piece of paper found a few days after his death, Bolton summed it up:

I felt what I felt
Were parts of me
Starting to fall apart.
Outside, the bare tree
Shivered, and the black birds
Shivered in the bare tree.

I was afraid to walk out
And pick up the morning paper
Till well into the night.
. . . .
And I was afraid to open up
The paper and read of a world
That had stopped having

Anything at all to do
With me, unless it be
News of my own death.

The voice in Bolton's work became, for me, the voice of
everyone who has ever asked, "Isn't there a chance it's we
who require revision? How green do the grass, the trees have
to get before you begin?" As I read him, I knew his depression
was imperative; I also knew that his suicide was (and mine
would be) a mistake. It was not wrong or immoral; it was
simply a mistake, irrevocable and immutable. In "Weightlifter
Poems," he writes:

202 ANIMAL MINERAL RADICAL

Not of cancer, not of old age,
But suddenly—
As when the bar slips
And the iron comes crashing through my chest
Like the shrunken planet through some unlucky ceiling.

And I will be the man
No one remembers,
Who won't be able to tell them—
Even if he knew—whether it's worth,
After all, the strength it takes to carry on.

———————

A year or so after the earthquake, I could answer with certainty, *Yes, it is worth it.* On the other side of depression, life is unequivocally worth living. It is a certainty I first glimpsed in the moment the earth shook, and the power of connection that grazed me then is what gave me the strength to carry on.

———————

It took me a year to find a new home after the quake. When I did, I uprooted the carpet of green lawn that surrounded the place. I tilled the soil and planted anything, everything native to that land. I wanted to give something back to the sweet black dirt that had saved me. I worked late into the night, gardening by moonlight. The cool earth felt like clay, and I felt like a potter creating something lasting, but delicate. With the night chill brushing across my skin, I planted seeds of food I would eat, flowers that offered beauty as essential to my spirit as food was to my belly, and bushes that would provide shade and nests to birds and other animals.

I dug to the bottom of my compost pit where the corn husks, melon rinds, and apple cores turned to a dark, unidentifiable muck. I lifted my shovel and carried my own private muck to a hole in the ground where it would provide nutrients for that year's miniharvest.

As I worked, I relaxed into the solace that my body, someday, would become like this rich compost that offered so much continuing possibility. As for my spirit, it was already biodegrading, a sort of mythical centaur, half human, half earth, and that felt good to me.

⋅•⊰⋅⋅•⊱•⋅

The Loma Prieta (which means "dark ridge") had picked me up, shaken me, and dropped me right smack-dab in the middle of geologic time. I saw that my life was merely a blip in the evolution of this huge and powerful thing called the earth—and I was grateful. Every morning, I woke up before dawn and counted my reasons for living: the trees, the scent of the ocean, the morning air, the night air, the air. I recited these reasons like prayers—no longer prayers of desperation, but of gratitude. I listened to the sound of the ocean rising and falling, a constant motion beneath the surface, reshaping loss.

"Plate Tectonics and Other Underground Theories of Loss" update: In this essay, I do not mean to discourage others from taking pharmaceutical antidepressants. This kind of ecopsychology worked for me. But depression is a serious condition and exploring all available options is essential.

Joe Bolton's poetry, from The Last Nostalgia: Poems 1982–1990, *is reprinted with the permission of the University of Arkansas Press. Copyright © 1999 by Ed Bolton.*

WORD HOARD

Once, I became aphasic. "Synapses," one of my doctors explained to me, "are an all-or-none proposition." Mine were none.

Fish: *Bagel*.

Lion: *Table*.

Pelican: *Funicular*.

This is the way I named things. *The funicular skimmed the surface of the ocean searching for bagels. Ocean* was big enough, usually, to fit on my tongue and palate, to dance on my tongue and groove. The rest of the words I have filled in after the fact, like we usually do with memory (aphasic or not). We like to be understood. What I really might have said may have involved *funicular* and *bagel*, but the words between would have been gibberish. My brain was an unplanned language poem, and I a woman who disliked language poetry for its insistence upon ambiguity. When you don't have it, language becomes unflinchingly precise.

Signifier: Signified: Bullshit.

Words carry on their backs their entire histories. This is what I learned the day they packed up and left me languageless. No forwarding address, no wish-you-were-here postcard.

Postcard: *Night Cream*.

Yard: *Breast.*

Water: *Orgasm.*

Fuck me. I was dead in the water without language.

As it is with any lover, I did not see my words packing their bags to go. If I had, I'd have tried to stop them. I'd have begged, "Let's work this out, you and me. Let's find a middle ground."

I did not see the verbs colluding with the nouns, the adverbs separating off, the adjectives running like lemmings to the cliff of my lips. I went to bed one night with a congregation gathering in my throat to sing me awake the next morn, and I woke with a stale mix of nonsense in my mouth, Froot Loops instead of the promise of eggs hatching thoughts in my brain for breakfast.

My doctors were flummoxed.

A year into it, and I was depressed. I do not mean sad. I mean looking for the word *gun* daily, something to put in my mouth.

I had studied classics instead of writing in college. I needed to know the genetic origin of words. Their family tree. I mean, without that, all words are adopted. They grow up angry foster children wanting to burn things down. I wanted to know their mother and grandmother. I wanted to know their Adam, their Eve, their Eden, their original sin. Knowledge.

When you use the word *flummox*, for instance, your tongue rolls across the same territory of every person who has ever spoken that word. They say that every third breath you breathe contains at least one of the same molecules Caesar exhaled as he was dying. Muriel Rukeyser has said *The universe is made of stories, not atoms*. Think of words, then, the same words you breathe that have been inhaled and exhaled throughout history. If you're looking for a link, there it is. They are only shapes and noises formed into meaning. But how many shapes and noises have crossed the tongues of those who have come before? And this exact shape and noise has crossed centuries to come to you now, fully formed, Athena from Zeus's head (or so you believe as it transforms itself even as it leaves your lips).

Words say simultaneously too much and too little. This is why they're perfect for communication, most people's lives operating in the balance between too much and too little. Nothing more precise.

In those years without language, I was limbless. I had no way to reach out. I had no way to touch others or myself. Water: *Orgasm*. My body had no reason to come or go anywhere.

Words are my nourishment. They are the molecules that seethe in my veins. They are the light that filters through the rods and cones of my eyes to create color and dimension. They are my resting heart rate, my tulips, my knives, my forks, and my spoons.

Writing, to me, means food, means sustenance. If I had another choice, I tell you, I would make money. It's a Catch-22. You must eat to live, must live to work. I eat my art for breakfast because I know what it is to go wordless, to be naked on the tongue and groping for a story that makes sense.

Towel: *Meridian*.

Apple: *Bird*.

Chalice: *Fly*.

Write: *Live*.

Silence: *Die*.

It's a cliché. But here's what I know. I have come into existence alongside words. Others have come into existence alongside business or sculpture or engineering or music or acting or science. But words carry with them a unique challenge. We use them daily, whether we love them or not. And so, loving them is a fix. Unless you are stuck in a Hollywood musical, people do not usually sing as a form of communication. Unless you are Neanderthal, they do not usually draw. But people will talk to you with words even when you are a writer. They will toss your medium around willy-nilly. They will use it to bad ends. They will use it to create wars, to manipulate leaders, to rape people, to sell.

You will be tempted to think your medium mundane, sometimes evil. You will be forced to discipline yourself against this. It will make you poor.

Once, I was aphasic. The condition lasted, to some extent or another, ten years. When I came back to words I came back like a lover who'd had a mistaken affair. Once the damage is done, it's done. But there is a carefulness that follows. You don't take things for granted. You speak from the soles of your feet, a current of meaning running through your body, each word carrying with it its history and the intimate mouths of your ancestors speaking it. Their lips touch yours as the word leaves you.

This is what connects you to who you are. What you love. What you caress. Whatever it is that leaves you and in its absence, makes you lonelier than God.

When it returns, it becomes holy. When it returns, you see the sacred in the profane. You do not fall prostrate before it. You hold it. You let it go. You live with it. You live.

GRATITUDE

Lisa Cech, you know the words I often say, and you know how they fall short. When I lost words, you listened to me all the same. You were the tectonic shift in my life that shook me home.

Doreen and Joe Piellucci, you give my words a wingspan that their feathers alone could never dream of. Besides that, there's this friendship we have. I hold it dear. See you at Kenny's.

Jack Shoemaker, as long as you're working in this business, there will be books full of words written with patience and care, book covers with beautiful images, and pages filled with humanity. Your integrity is stunning, Jack. Thanks to all my editors at Counterpoint.

Barbara Sloan Jordan, Verna Sloan, and Don Jordan. Here's a huge thank you for always being there over the decades and across the distance.

Mary-Gaye Kinsala and Beth Bogner, you make my hometown a home. We share cooking, skiing, dogs, music, and you read my work with patience and intelligence. What's more, you bring your whole fam damily into it: Kathryn and Mother Mary, you are two of my go-to readers, and your friendship is golden. Boob (yup, Boob), Susan, Barbara, you're my go-to gals for laughs, games, reading, and good old home-style food. See you at the next BBQ.

Ann Pancake, Sarah Saffian (my homeslice!), Kelly Dwyer, Juliet Patterson, Lisa Cech, Susan Taylor Chehak, Aina Barten, Chip Blake, Harry Greene, Doreen Piellucci, Sheryl St. Germaine, and someone I am no doubt forgetting (apologies), thank you for your careful reading of early versions of these essays, or for your support of the finished pieces, and thanks, most of all, for your friendship.

Tattered Cover, you great good place, thank you. And thanks to independent bookstores and booksellers everywhere. Charles, you know you're at the top of this list.

Liz Darhansoff, you've made all the difference. Thanks, as ever.

Lauren Bishop-Weidner and Ellen Pinkham, you get a line of your own, just because. I can't sum up the reason for my gratitude; you'll just have to trust it. It's huge.

To Susan Booker, Rachel Hanson, and the PAC/LCAC crew in Lafayette, thanks for engulfing this corner of the world in art and compassion.

To my dogs and cats: No matter what I write here or what I say to you when you're in the room, you won't be able to understand my gibberish. We communicate clearly and with love all the same. So much for the necessity of words.

To my readers: Thank you for every moment you have spent with these words. Thank you for you. And thanks to you for keeping independent bookstores alive.

On my father's last day of life, I wheeled my mom into my dad's hospital room. His spine was broken and she could not stand. I had to lower my dad's bed, tilt the wheelchair, and then help Mom stand without getting in the way of what they knew would be their last kiss after sixty-five years of marriage. I wheeled my mother out of the room and she called back, "I love you." My dad said very softly, just the words, "You know, Marge."

To Mom and Dad: You know.

REPRINT ACKNOWLEDGMENTS

"Trends of Nature" first appeared as "Coyotes" in *Alligator Juniper*, volume 6, 2000. It was revised and retitled, "Trends of Nature," and first published in that form in *Between Song and Story: Essays for the 21st Century,* Sheryl St. Germaine and Margaret Whitford (Autumn House Press, June 2011).

"The Shifting Light of Shadows" first appeared in *Listening to Cougar*, Marc Bekoff and Cara Blessley Lowe (Boulder: University of Colorado Press, 2008).

"Of Straw Dogs and Canines: A Meditation on Place" first appeared as "What It Is That Feeds Us" in *Orion Magazine*, July/August 2010, and was reprinted in *Best Spiritual Writing of 2012*, ed. Philip Zaleski (New York: Penguin Books, 2011).

"Margie's Discount" first appeared in *Dutiful Daughters*, ed. Jean Gould (Seattle: Seal Press, 1999).

"Fighting Time" first appeared in *The Way of the River*, BK Loren (Guilford, Connecticut: Lyons Press, an imprint of Globe-Pequot, 2001).

"Snapshots of My Redneck Brother" first appeared in *Orion Magazine*, March/April 2007.

"The Evolution of Hunger" was first published in *Hawk and Handsaw: The Journal of Creative Sustainability,* a publication of Unity College of Maine, Fall 2012.

"Back Words" first appeared as "I Would Like To Be a Fool" in *Parabola, the Magazine of Myth and Tradition*, volume 26, number 3, Fall 2001.

"Learning Fear" first appeared in *The Way of the River*, BK Loren (Guilford, Connecticut: Lyons Press, an imprint of Globe-Pequot, 2001).

"Got Tape" first appeared in *Orion Magazine*, May/June 2003.

"This Little Piggy Stayed Home" was originally published as "Odd Shaped Tomatoes" in *Spirituality and Health*, July/August 2008.

"Plate Tectonics and Other Underground Theories of Loss" was originally published in *Orion Magazine*, Autumn 1999.

"Word Hoard" was originally published in *Parabola, the Magazine of Myth and Tradition*, volume 8, number 3, August 2003; it was reprinted in *Best American Spiritual Writing of 2004*, ed. Philip Zaleski (New York: Houghton-Mifflin, 2003).

NOTES

INTRODUCTION

1. "Please RT," nplusonemag.com, June 14, 2012.
2. John Fowles, *The Tree* (New York: Harper Collins; Ecco Reprint Edition, 2010), 47.
3. John Fowles, *The Tree,* 42.

TRENDS OF NATURE

1. Horace Miner, "Body Ritual Among the Nacirema," in *The Nacirema: Readings on American Culture*, ed. James P. Spradley and Michael A. Rynkiewich (Boston: Little, Brown and Company, 1975), 10.
2. Neil B. Thompson, "The Mysterious Fall of the Nacirema," in *The Nacirema: Readings on American Culture*, ed. James P. Spradley and Michael A. Rynkiewich (Boston: Little, Brown and Company, 1975), 412.

THE SHIFTING LIGHT OF SHADOWS

1. Carl Gustav Jung, "The Philosophical Tree," paragraph 335, in *Alchemical Studies, Collected Works Volume 13*, trans. R. F. C. Hull (Princeton, New Jersey: Princeton University Press, 1967), 265.

FIGHTING TIME

1. Thomas H. Maugh II, "Chemicals Called Main Cause of Parkinson's," *Los Angeles Times*, January 27, 1999. See www.latimes.com/HOME/NEWS/SCIENCE/ENVIRON/t000008230.html Also see "Pesticides Impact on Human Health," www.pmac.net/parkinson.html.
2. Sandra Steingraber, *Living Downstream* (New York: Random House, 1997), 60–61.
3. David Ehrenfeld, "Pretending," *Orion Magazine*, Autumn 2000.
4. Harvey Wasserman and Norman Solomon, *Killing Our Own* (New York: Dell Publishing Company, 1982), 261.
5. Harvey Wasserman and Norman Solomon, *Killing Our Own*, 261.
6. "Currently" in this paragraph refers to the year 1999, when I wrote this essay. It is now 2013, and the hiking trails have been completed. The area is called "Rocky Flats National Wildlife Refuge." A topo map of its trails includes a gray area with zero contour lines and labeled "Department of Energy Retained Area." www.fws.gov/rockyflats/images/rfl_LandStatus_071911-1000.jpg.
7. Harvey Wasserman and Norman Solomon, *Killing Our Own*, throughout.

THE EVOLUTION OF HUNGER

1. Reay Tannahill, *Food in History* (New York: Three Rivers Press, 1988), 3.

2. Reay Tannahill, *Food in History*, 3.

3. Raey Tannahill, *Food in History,* 1.

4. Jeff Hecht, "Chimps are Human, Gene Study Implies," *New Scientist*, www.newscientist.com/article/dn3744-chimps-are -human-gene-study-implies.html, May 19, 2003.

5. "Implications of natural selection in shaping 99.4% nonsynonymous DNA identity between humans and Chimpanzees: Enlarging genus *Homo*," Proceedings of the National Academy of the Sciences of the United States of America, contributed by Morris Goodman, www.pnas.org/ content/100/12/7181.abstract, April 14, 2003.

6. Laura Schenone, *A Thousand Years Over a Hot Stove* (New York: W.W. Norton and Company, 2003), 118.

THIS LITTLE PIGGY STAYED HOME

1. UMassAmherst, "CSA Information and Listings," http://extension.umass.edu/vegetable/resources/ csa-information-listings.